ExtraVagan t
Fire

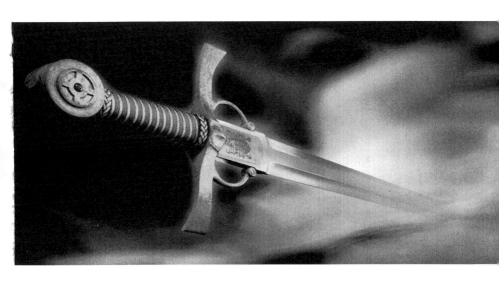

Sue Sinclair

First Edition - March 2014

Front cover image: Judah Cole: www.judahcoledesign.com
All rights reserved

Sue Sinclair can be contacted at cwmprayer@me.com
Her ministry website is: www.cwmprayer.com

ISBN 978-1-908154-10-1
Printed in the United Kingdom

CONTENTS

ACKNOWLEDGMENTS

I honour my precious husband Steve who has been my best friend since we were 14 and 15 years old and my husband since 1979. He has stood with me throughout the good times and the turbulent times. Steve has had the wisdom to help me to walk away when my faithful heart would have caused me to remain in relationships that were abusive and destructive.

I thank my wonderful children who are a precious gift in my life.

I applaud my great friends Norma Dean, Tina and Colin Grant, Pam Shaw, Jean Dodd and the wonderful Community Watchmen Ministries Team. They have provoked and made time for me to complete Extravagant Fire. Thankfully at times they have actually walked through the midst of the fire with me.

Special thanks to David Powell, Judah and Rachel Cole, Michael Marcel, Ann Weaver, Rosemary Burden and Liz Geddes for your friendship and for assisting me in the process of completing this book.

I thank Jesus, who in 1985 said He would never leave me or forsake me, and He never has and He never will!

The Lord himself goes before you and will be with you; he will never leave you nor forsake you. Do not be afraid; do not be discouraged. Deuteronomy 31:8

ENDORSEMENTS

"I first met Sue in 2002 and am honoured that she has become a very precious and special friend. Her story is so encouraging. It clearly shows how God can take a broken life into His hands and mould and fashion it into a beautiful vessel that can bring honour to Him. God has allowed Sue to go through many testing times but only so that she can become stronger and more reliant on Him. Sue's story will inspire you to stand firm in the storms of life so that you can reach your destiny and become all that you are intended to be."

Norma Dean
Community Watchmen Ministries

"Life is a journey of choices. In this heartfelt and honest book Sue shares her personal story, challenging the reader to recognise that even when circumstances are against you - God is still for you. From the trauma of growing up in an alcoholic home, to the struggle of raising a family through times of unemployment and financial struggle, this book covers life but challenges you to forgive and rebuild with Jesus. Even when the church failed to recognise the cry of the little girl seeking God, we read the account of the faithfullness of God, who speaks anyway. This book will awaken your gratitude to an amazing God that loves to set people free for purpose. In the times of extreme pressure and confusion God never fails and this extravagant fire of God's love burns with HOPE! Through these TESTING FIRES a story of PURPOSE is born, so ENJOY a good read."

Rachel Hickson
Heartcry for Change – Director and Founder.

"As I read Extravagant Fire I marvelled at Sue's vulnerability and God's amazing grace. I also realized what courage it took Sue to write this book as many of her family are still living. I also was encouraged by how one life can make a territorial difference. I believe you will fall in love with God all over again as you read this book and you will be empower to bring change."

Dr Sharon Stone
Christian International Europe

"In this book we see the story behind the woman and the ministry. We read about the incredible journey that Sue has been on over the years, and we see God's calling on her life, and how He has walked with Sue on this journey through the challenges and the joys of life. As you read these pages you see God's grace bringing healing to a broken heart, enabling her to operate at an intimate level of knowing the Father's heart. God has given Sue insight into different areas over the years, and many opportunities to proclaim His goodness and truth all over the world. Read this book and be encouraged."
Dave Connolly
Senior Pastor Frontline Church

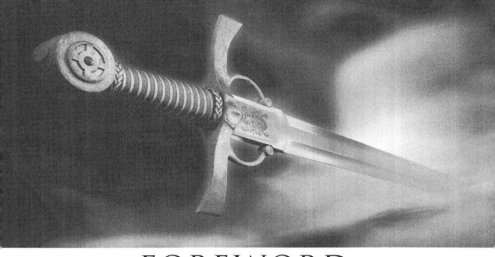

FOREWORD

MARTIN SCOTT

If you love to read then you will enjoy what is in your hands. You will probably pick it up and devour the words that are inside it. Sue writes with a straightforwardness, a simplicity and a depth of honesty that makes what one reads very accessible. This book makes for a great read and my hope is that many will pick this book up and read Sue's story. However, this is more than a great read, and it is more than the story of someone's life and experience. For this reason I pray that this book will be read by thousands who will find a deep resonation with her story.

The chapters unfold Sue's history. As readers, we probably all approach a book differently. As I read it I stopped, shook my head as I reflected, read on, turned the page, found places of personal resonance but as the story developed found myself being deeply thankful to God for the transformation and hope that he brings. Hope can so easily elude us and we can end up in a place of discouragement or even a dark place. We can try to counteract our discouragement many ways with various levels of success. In the pages of Extravagant Fire you will be provoked, challenged, but there is something that runs through it that you will 'feel', dare I say it, like a substance, like a 'thing', like a constant flow toward you. I am not sure how you will describe it, but for me, it was a warmth, a 'keep going it is going to be OK' kind of settledness. It was what I have already written in the first paragraph, a resonance that took place inside.

This is why I pray this book will impact the lives of many. You are not about to read the story of someone who is writing for personal therapy, nor someone who is writing triumphantly. Sue writes honestly as she knows what it is to be in deep waters when to keep one's head above the waters is as much as one can hope for. She does not skirt around her personal history. In her vulnerability she communicates that God was not far distant but was deeply present for her, shaping her life. I am more convinced after reading the book that God's healing is not simply to take us out of a situation, but to come to us in a situation, to give us hope and to transform us. What he does in us is certainly what he will do through us.

I look forward to subsequent books from Sue, in which we will be able to read of the remarkable answers to prayer at a corporate, city and national level, but this is where it all starts. It does not begin with what she has been involved in, but who she is, and about the God who is involved with her. I have sat many times with her and heard some remarkable stories of answered prayer. I have copies of letters from people who are not yet believers testify to the difference that prayer has made when they have had encounters with Sue or the team she works with. I have told the same stories to others and I absolutely love to recount such stories. I hope we see many of those stories in print in the future. A few of those stories are inside, however I am thankful that we do not simply have a set of stories but a recounting at a personal level of a personal journey.

I do not know how to describe Sue. I sometimes refer to her as 'an ordinary lady from Liverpool' That is true. She is no superstar. She is not arrogant nor carries an ego. She is ordinary. Yet she is a testimony to how it is possible to discover who you really are at the core, and how God can place you in the right place at the right time. Each time I have had contact with Sue I have left encouraged and had the same experience when reading this manuscript.

If the era of the superstar is over, that we are in a time when a multitude of ordinary people will be involved in a multitude of small things that God will make significant, then this book will be one means through which some will find a healing for the past and a repositioning for their own release.

Hence my prayer that this book will be read by thousands.

Martin Scott
Writer and speaker

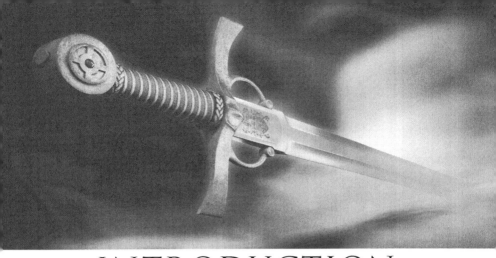

INTRODUCTION

I have been challenged to write this book for several years after many prophetic words and words of encouragement. I would be disobedient not to write it but I have to say in writing this I have been challenged by many questions and issues.

In any story what is the truth? Our story as we see it is only our perception of what has happened, filtered through our experience, character and attitudes. So I start on my journey of writing this in the hope that my perception of the truth is wholesome and will be an honest reflection. I know that my God is the God of reconciliation, healing and breakthroughs. God never ceases to amaze me in the way He loves to use very ordinary people to accomplish that.

I believe that as you read this - Jesus is going to speak to you and challenge you in many different ways. I know He has challenged me! I hope that my experiences and the things Jesus has taught me along the way will help you to avoid some of the mistakes I have made and to overcome any traumas you are struggling with. Maybe too, this book will give you the courage to stand, when it seems impossible naturally to stand and to enable you to arise into your destiny.

This is the first of two books I am writing. In the second book, Extravagant Adventures, I will tell the many amazing stories of how God has used me and the CWM team around the world in some incredible ways. He has opened doors that would normally be closed to Mum from Liverpool!

But first my journey through the Fire of God and into those adventures.

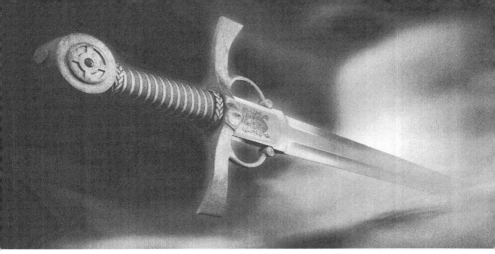

EXTRAVAGANT FIRE

Have you ever witnessed the scenes of controlled burning, sometimes also known as prescribed burning? It often takes places in forest areas to reduce the amount of dead vegetation and to decrease the risk of bushfires that could cause greater damage later on. The extensive and damaging fires in Australia and Los Angeles are fearsome examples of what can go wrong when wild fires ravage the countryside and destroy everything in their paths.

The controlled burning is all done under supervision to ensure that only what needs to be destroyed is removed and is seen as a positive tool for foresters. Studies have actually revealed that something is released through these fires that germinates many seeds that have been laying dormant in the ground, sometimes for many years. The seeds lie there hidden in the ground, full of potential for life, just waiting for the fire to come.

Once the fire is extinguished, having done its job destroying all the dead wood and rot it makes room for the new life to come. It is surprising just how quickly the seed bursts into life. The only way plants like this could have a reliance on fire was for God to have designed them that way from the very beginning.

I witnessed this first hand several times out in Uganda where the authorities choose to set fire to specific areas. They do this to burn up the dead and rotting vegetation that is no longer fruitful or purposeful. If they chose not to carry out these controlled burns there could either be total devastation if a wild fire broke out, or the animals that need the new growth for food would go hungry.

As soon as the fires start, birds of all sizes and breeds gather from miles around. They come to make the most of the opportunity for the rich pickings of insects that had been breeding in the midst of the rot and decay of the dead vegetation. As the fire travels, the birds position themselves so close to the edge of the fire. In fact, I don't know how they don't get roasted, but I'm sure they must get their feet scorched! However they are an important part of the process of regeneration, as they eat all that could hamper the future new growth. This controlled fire brings life and that is why I believe it is extravagant fire.

In our lives we have seasons when the extravagant fire of God touches us - when it's the fire of God it is started and controlled by Him. The good news is that God does not abandon us during these times, but he actually walks through the fire with us and in fact, sometimes He actually carries us through.

His fire comes, burning up our dead wood and exposing the rot that can be hidden in our lives. Wounded people can so often end up full of bitterness and anger, which can cause more problems, leading to more wounding for them and others. The rot can develop quickly or over many years when we have not allowed the Lord to cleanse and heal those wounds. Often we simply need to come close enough to allow God to pour His love into our lives.

Sometimes we need to say we are sorry for things we have done wrong that have contributed to us being wounded. This is called repentance and is a very powerful way to deal with the rot. We might need to do that in person, by a telephone call or through a card, but that is not always possible. It helps if we say we are sorry to God too! Another powerful and essential tool is forgiveness, as this actually sets us free and helps us not to keep revisiting the wound.

The bugs and insects that the birds feed on, represent the battle that goes on in our minds. We often hear that little voice that replays what has happened, over and over again. Allow the Lord to help you to deal with all those negative thoughts as soon as they come. Do not brood over what has happened, keep your eyes on the Lord and He will bring you through the fire, even stronger than before.

When we yield to the fire of God, we always experience new life and growth. Often these times can re-direct the course of our lives, impacting those around us and can even change nations.

A great example of this was in the story of Moses, told throughout the book of Exodus. He was born in Egypt at a dangerous time as Pharaoh had ordered all the Hebrew baby boys to be destroyed. When he was just a few months old, His mother had arranged for him to be hidden in reed beds of the River Nile, in order to protect him from slaughter. However he was found by Pharaoh's daughter and raised within Pharaoh's palace. Years later, when Moses observed the brutality of the Egyptians towards his people, he attempted to bring freedom to them himself. He ended up killing an Egyptian and running for his life into the desert. Moses was born to lead but he had messed up big style!

Moses could have grown up angry, believing that his real mother had abandoned him. Even his attempt to bring freedom was despised even by his own people. He had been living like a Prince in Egypt and now he was left looking after the sheep and the goats in the desert – what a mess! However God had not finished with Moses, and many years later God appeared to him in the midst of a burning bush. His attention was drawn to God by the fire and although feeling totally incapable, he responded to God's call to lead the Hebrew people into freedom.

Moses chose to yield to the fire of God. As a result, instead of leading sheep and goats through the desert, he became one of the greatest leaders ever known. God used him to bring freedom to a whole nation, through performing the most amazing miracles, from turning the River Nile into blood, to leading the Hebrews as they walked across the Red Sea on dry ground. Through Moses, God provided food and water for the multitudes but greater than that, he was used to turn a nation back to God and His plans for them.

That is the extravagant fire of God and it changes everything it touches!

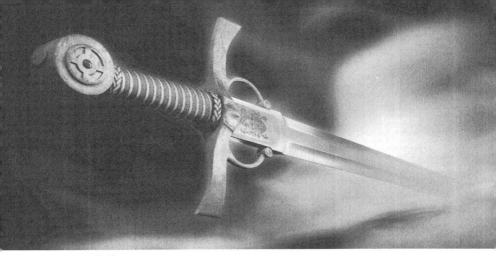

KEY IN THE DOOR

I would like to share with you how the extravagant fire of God has touched my life and to encourage you to trust God to allow Him to release it into your life too.

We start our lives with no experience and no choices. Born into a time in history, a family and geographical area completely of God's choosing and with complete confidence and trust in Him for our provision. How do I know that? I know because I love God's word. King David said:

> *For you created my inmost being; you knit me together in my mother's womb.* Psalm 139:13

Just in case you are not convinced God said this to the Prophet Jeremiah:

> *"Before I formed you in the womb I knew you, before you were born I set you apart; I appointed you as a prophet to the nations."* Jeremiah 1:5

It is overwhelming for us to consider that even before we are formed, God knows us and is confident in the plans He has for our lives. He has had a long time to get His plans right since we have been on His heart since before the earth was even created! In the history of eternity God knows just the time and the place for us to be born.

"For I know the plans I have for you," declares the Lord, *"plans to prosper you and not to harm you, plans to give you hope and a future."* Jeremiah 29:11

When we are born we have no concept of what we have been born into, whether we are born into the British royal family, into a poor family in the worst African slums or something in between. For many years we have no idea of how our life compares to those around us. We do not know if it is a good life or a problematic life. We have no understanding of what has gone before us through the generational lines of our parents or what kind of childhood they had. We also do not know the history of our land. However, we arrive in the correct place, at exactly the right moment in history destined by God. How awesome and how encouraging!

There is a time for everything, and a season for every activity under the heavens: a time to be born and a time to die. Ecclesiastes 3:1-2

I was the first child born into our family, arriving on 21st November 1959. My Mum was nineteen years old when she hurriedly married my Dad, and was only twenty when she gave birth to me. I was conceived before they were married and I was the first fruit of a very chaotic relationship.

Mum was twelve years old when her mother died, not long after her father had left the family for another woman. Mum and her brother were orphaned at a very vulnerable age and were raised by their Grandmother (a wonderful woman I believe). I do not think Mum ever recovered fully from the traumatic relationship with her Dad and from losing her mother at such a sensitive age.

Dad was one of the youngest of twelve children and had a dreadful and poverty stricken childhood. One of his brothers died when he was only a small child. His father was extremely cruel and I was once told of him setting fire to the house when his wife and all the children were asleep in bed. There was a rumour that he had written his autobiography that included stories of him having sexual relationships as a rent boy with army officers during the First World War. Dad's mother was a very hard woman too. I remember her getting a beautiful little puppy that she drowned in the bath a few weeks later, for laddering her stockings!

Damaged lives often damage lives and the result of their upbringing resulted in none of Dad's brothers and sisters managing to prosper and succeed in life. Most of those who did have children, watched them go very badly astray.

It was tough in those days and my Dad, like many young men of that era, escaped life at home by going into the army for national service. The army taught my Dad many disciplines, but one of the undesirable things he learnt was how to drink heavily.

Mum and Dad met and probably married for all the wrong reasons; two very hurt and confused young people thrown together as they looked desperately for love, without any healing or recovery from their past. Almost three years after I was born, my brother arrived and experienced some feeding problems that required urgent surgery.

Sadly, I do not have many memories of my life as a small child, although I am sure there were probably plenty of them. It is so sad that for many of us any good memories are often drowned out by the bad ones, but it does not mean we never had happy times. Most of my memories are from the age of around twelve when life for me seemed to take a painful and chaotic turn.

I have to confess that there were many times in the past when I wondered if God had made a huge mistake in birthing me into the world. I blamed myself, wrongly taking upon myself all the responsibility, believing that I was the cause of my parents' unhappiness.

My Dad did not drink alcohol all the time, but when he did he seemed incapable of consuming just a pint or two of beer. Whenever he drank it had to be until he was completely drunk and Mum often joined him in that process.

They would go out to a local club every Friday evening, where they would be the life and soul of the party. However, they would return home very drunk and usually violent. It would not take much to upset Dad and within minutes my brother and I would be woken from our sleep by shouting and screaming, followed by the sound of smashing and breaking. Many nights our terrified neighbours would call the Police on our behalf and they would arrive to find the house smashed up. The Police intervention would often result in Dad being taken away by the Police and it would take six or seven officers to handle him, as he was so violent. Mum would often be left in need of hospital attention and I would be left to call the ambulance and look after her.

In those days it was up to the victim to press charges. Due to the manipulation and control by the violent person, a victim would commonly believe that the trouble was all their fault. This is still a problem where there is domestic violence today, although thankfully the Police are now empowered to take action without the victim pressing charges. There is now a lot more help available for families and victims, but it still remains a huge problem.

Dad would often slip into a deep drunken sleep on the settee in the living room, making it out of bounds for any other use. The whole house would stink of stale cigarette smoke and strong alcohol. As youngsters we found it very scary as you could cut the atmosphere with a knife. We were terrified of waking him in case another fight would be started.

While our parents were enjoying their nights out, my brother and I would be cared for by people our parents knew. It was during that time that we were both sexually abused by one of them. Typical of this kind of abuse, my brother did not know what was happening to me and I did not know he was being abused either. We were told it was to be kept a secret and we maintained a crippled silence. As with most trauma of this nature, it was something that we never spoke about until many years later. Our parents were oblivious to what was going on at home by those they had trusted with our care, and I am sure that if they had been aware there would have been even more violence.

I am very sad to say that in the many counselling sessions I have ministered in over the years, so many people have spoken of similar and worse stories of sexual abuse. There are more victims of this than we will ever know about, as it is one of those secrets people never usually talk about. Instead we bury it alive, we live with the pain and the shame, believing that somehow we deserved it or it was our fault. What a lie! What a deception!

As a young teenager, watching my parents hurting each other both physically and mentally was a terrifying torture and a torment. Eventually it reached a point where my brother and I would be asleep in our bedrooms on Friday nights, and we would wake up petrified waiting for the violence to start, if it had not already, knowing we were about to be thrown into the middle of a fight we had not picked. I was always afraid that this would be the night when Dad would go too far and this would be the time when Mum would not survive the fight. Would this be the night when the Police would take Dad away and he would be imprisoned leaving my brother and me with no one to help us?

Mum and Dad would row almost every Friday night, with whatever consequences that brought with it. Then they would not speak to each other for several days, reconciling just before it was time for the dreaded night out again. As with most domestic violence relationships there would be sorrow and deep regret, accompanied by assurances that it would never happen again - but it always did.

The vicious cycle of our lives became more and more chaotic when one day my Dad was admitted into hospital. Mum took me to visit him but I cannot remember anyone telling me why he was there. Dad returned home and months later we would again be visiting him in hospital. There were several of these episodes before I discovered that he had been trying to kill himself. As a young teenager that came as a great shock to me and it simply added to the mountain of rejection and confusion that I was already feeling. You see my parents were so broken and busy just trying to get through the day, that they did not seem to notice how it was affecting their children.

People talk of the "demon drink" and I know that it certainly dwelt in our home. Often I would try to put myself between my parents to try to stop the violence but it was very terrifying. Dad would lose his temper so easily, often resulting in doors being broken and items around the house getting smashed. As the eldest child, it was usually left to me to call the ambulance and attend to my Mum. Often, she was so drunk herself that she was not able to make sense of what was happening and she would be left sobbing and covered in blood. Several times she had difficulty breathing and we thought she was having a heart attack. However we later discovered that these were panic attacks brought on by the fear and stress. Many times she would be left with a battered face, black eyes and a swollen nose. The humiliation, embarrassment and deep shame that I experienced stayed with me for many years.

During the days that followed the fighting, Mum would hide herself away in her bedroom and my brother and I would be left to pass messages between her and my Dad. My brother and I were constantly stuck in the middle - fearfully hoping that we had communicated things correctly between them and that we would not say anything that would stir things up all over again.

I remember Mum being admitted into hospital for some surgery and Dad was left in charge. However he went gambling and lost all the money. Life was tough for Mum but she did try her best to hold everything together.

Dad was a hard worker but very volatile and did not seem capable of controlling his temper. One day, Dad's boss spoke to him aggressively and Dad was not best pleased. This resulted in him throwing a knife at his boss which thankfully missed! He was fired from his job, which again put great pressure on our family.

My brother was very clever and was sent to a private school. Despite him getting a scholarship to go it was still very expensive. Maybe that was one of the reasons my brother and I did not get on so well together. He had tasted another world that certainly gave him hopes and dreams of a better and more prosperous life and who could blame him for wanting that?

I felt constantly rejected by my Dad and my brother, feeling that I was never good enough, no matter how hard I tried to please them. As a child and young person, I cannot ever remember anyone telling me they loved me or even giving me a cuddle. I grew up hurting, angry and full to the brim with rejection, plus I was burdened with responsibilities that were not mine to bear.

I was thirteen years old when I went to the local church hoping that someone there would be able to help or even just listen. Sadly I did not find any help there at all and I was told you do not talk about what goes on inside your home! I was broken and unable to bear the huge weight of responsibility that had fallen on to my shoulders. Overwhelmed, one day I took an overdose and ended up in Alder Hey Children's Hospital where they pumped my stomach to eject the tablets from my body. They kept me in hospital overnight but nobody seemed to care that I was so unhappy and no one attempted to find out what was going wrong in my life. I felt very lonely, confused and isolated.

Around that time I would go on shoplifting sprees and steal lots of make-up that I hid in a drawer in my bedroom. I hated myself for doing it but could not seem to stop. Thankfully, one day I was stopped coming out of a shop with make-up I had not paid for. I was relieved when the Police were called and they took me home. I was given a warning but once again my cries for attention were not recognised and nobody ever spoke of it again. Thankfully it did stop me from shoplifting or stealing ever again.

School was a lonely place where I felt remote and very unhappy. I was bullied because I was tall for my age and during a netball lesson, I was pushed onto the ground by a group of girls. This left me with my elbow torn open and pouring with blood from a gaping wound. The timing was not good, as unfortunately this happened on my brother's birthday. He had some of his friends around for tea, so I was not taken to hospital until much later. As the wound was not attended to effectively, it became infected and did not heal properly.

A few weeks later my elbow required surgery. I was thirteen when I was taken into hospital where a male doctor gave me a breast examination, which was totally inappropriate and I burned with humiliation and embarrassment. Why was I having a breast examination for an operation on my elbow? I was too scared and ashamed to say anything. I wondered what was wrong with me that men thought they had a right to touch me in ways that men should not touch young teenagers or any woman for that matter. I was riddled with guilt and shame so I never spoke about it for many years.

Young people with alcohol problems is not a new thing. It was that at the age of thirteen I began drinking and would smuggle cider or other bottles out from Mum's supply. It would not take a lot to get me drunk and life seemed so much better when I was in a drunken stupor. It blotted everything out of my mind and lifted the burden of the responsibility off my shoulders for a little while. I would go all giggly and then simply fall into a deep sleep. I must have done a good job of hiding my drinking as nobody seemed to notice or if they did they chose to ignore it.

Life was lonely, made worse because it was almost impossible to bring friends home, as life there was so unstable. I felt isolated and afraid – my only comfort was my Auntie Eileen. She was a wonderful lady who sadly had never been able to have children of her own. Auntie Eileen was happy to welcome my brother and me into her life and was the only person who seemed to care about what was happening to us.

One day, Auntie Eileen had a terrible accident whilst in work. She had been lifting boxes when she slipped a disc in her spine and ended up in hospital. Things got very complicated for her when she had meningitis and then septicaemia, eventually resulting in her being very badly disabled and permanently in a wheelchair. She was brave and courageous, never flinching despite her terrible pain and loss of mobility. But tragically after battling her health problems for ten years, she died suddenly whilst in hospital for respite.

This was my first experience of death and I was completely heartbroken. I was angry that Auntie Eileen had been such a great lady and had suffered so badly. I was also angry that I had missed an opportunity to say "goodbye" to her. My first experience of emotions towards God was furious anger. After all what kind of God would allow this to happen to such a wonderful lady? If God had taken my Auntie Eileen in this way, after so much suffering, then He was not a God I wanted to know anything about!

Many people never recover from the traumas that damaged their childhood. If you are reading this and know that you too are one of those people - choose today to no longer be a victim. My wonderful Saviour took upon Himself all my sin, guilt and shame and made a way for me to be healed and to be free - really free.

The choice is simple but we complicate life far too much. Do not go on your feelings, as they will keep you trapped in pain and anger. We should choose to forgive those who have hurt us so badly and release them with a blessing. That way we do not necessarily forget what has happened to us, but we do not remain as victims or end up full of destructive bitterness and anger.

It really helped me to forgive my parents when I paused to understand their childhoods and their broken lives.

If you are struggling to forgive there are many helpful books and ministries available to help you through the process. In the Appendix I have included the names of some of these ministries.

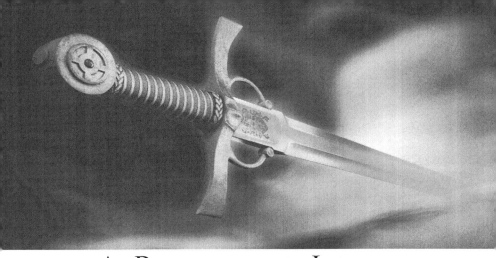

A PRECIOUS LOVE

During a school trip to see the mask of Tutankhamen in London, I met my beloved Steve. He was almost a year younger than me. I was fifteen years old and Steve was fourteen, and we fell in love with each other almost instantly. He was (and still is) the joy of my life and he gave me the ability to keep living, despite no changes in my home environment. Although my Dad was jealous and angry towards him, Steve stood by me. Many young men would have run a mile to get away as quickly as possible and who would have blamed them!

As I studied for my final school examinations there was no difference in the chaotic lifestyle at home. Nights were marked by drunken violence and sleepless nights. The night before my final examinations was spent with the Police once again taking Dad away. I went into school having worked very hard in my preparations but with a heavy, tired head and a broken heart. The fact that I managed to pass any examinations at all was an incredible miraculous gift from God, even though I did not realise it at the time. However, the constant pressure was too much for me and I could not face going on to College, as previously planned. Instead I settled for getting a job that provided on the job training and maybe a way out of our family home.

When I left school I worked for the local council, first in the Planning Department and then in Social Services. Steve worked for the Council too. However, the level of stress at home due to my Dad's violent behaviour was simply too much for me to bear and not long after I was eighteen years old, I left home. With nowhere to go, I walked out of our family home leaving my parents and younger brother behind and determined not to go back.

Steve's Mum and Dad took me in, initially on a temporary basis, whilst we looked for somewhere safe for me to live. I shared a bedroom with Steve's sisters who kindly made room for me. We searched for accommodation but there was nothing suitable. All that my meagre budget could afford were very grotty bedsits. Steve's Mum visited the bedsits with me and would not allow me to stay in any of them. So Steve's parents took me in for as long as I needed. I am so grateful to them to this day, as without them I do not know where I would have ended up, and grateful also to Steve's sisters for giving me space in their room.

While continuing to work full-time, I attended College part-time for one day and one evening a week where I met a precious friend, Linda Jones (now Hawksley) who is a lovely Christian. Often at College Linda would take opportunities, as they arose, to talk to me about Jesus. However I was a very angry young woman and probably gave Linda a difficult time but she never gave up on me. I ranted, asking how a loving God could allow my Auntie Eileen to suffer the way that she had. Linda of course had no clever answers, but she simply allowed me to get my hurt and anger out and loved me. Linda was a great Ambassador for Jesus and still is! We have been good friends since that time and I honour her.

My parents hated the fact that I had left and I had no real contact from them for many months, until Steve asked me to marry him and we began to make the arrangements for the wedding. We had a simple wedding in July 1979 with my Dad threatening not to give me away and to start a big fight. Thankfully the day passed without any major disturbance.

We began our married life living in a single bed in the box room of Steve's parents home. We did not care as long as we could be together and thankfully we were both a lot slimmer in those days! Steve and I lived like that for nine months before we managed to rent a little terraced house of our own.

We hoped that it would mark a new start for us, but my Dad started coming around late at night. He would appear at our door drunk, complete with a half empty bottle of alcohol, threatening violence against us and to smash our windows if we did not let him in. I would do my best to empty his bottle out whilst he visited the bathroom and to try to sober him up before he went home to Mum. Sometimes that worked, but mostly he would go home ready to start a fight. I always felt the burden of responsibility - would this be the night when he went too far and killed my Mum?

After several months of this, Steve and I decided we needed a fresh start and moved to Kent to train as Managers for Berni Inns Steak Houses. We were young, under lots of pressure and did not realise that actually we were running away! We started our training in The Wig and Gown in Maidstone, an old coaching inn with three bars and two restaurants, situated opposite the courts and prison.

We made some very interesting friends! This included "Shot-gun Dave" who was a local gangland leader. Dave offered us his hand of friendship after we took care of him in his time of need. Dave's wife had worked for us as a barmaid and she left him for a soldier from the local army barracks, whom she had met in the bar. As you can imagine Dave was very angry! So angry in fact, that he actually broke into the army camp to look for them, brandishing a sawn off shotgun.

Thankfully Dave did not find them, but he lost custody of his beloved boys. His wife was too afraid to meet him, so the Police arranged an exchange of the children at Maidstone Train Station (this was opposite The Wig and

Gown). Soon after, on a very rainy day, Dave had to hand his children over and the boys then left with their Mum on the train. Long after the train and the Police had gone, Dave stood there soaked to the skin because of the heavy rain, with tears pouring down his face.

He may have been a gangster but he was also a loving Dad who had lost his children. Steve and I had compassion on him, brought him in and dried him off. From that time on, he promised us that should we ever need anybody knee-capping, he would sort it for us. Needless to say we have never taken him up on that generous offer!

Berni Inns was a great training place for us for all that was to come. For example, I had my first experience with a microphone - ten minutes before the bars closed we had to make an announcement "Ladies and Gentlemen it is now last orders in the bar, last orders in the bar." Every time this had to be done I was so scared of the microphone, I would hide myself as far away as possible. I would busy myself in the hope that nobody would notice that I had avoided it again.

But the day came when our Managers declared I had to do it and I was so scared! The microphone was tucked into the corner of the bar, so I gripped it with both hands, tucking myself as far into the corner as I could. Embarrassed, I turned my back to everyone in the room so nobody could see my bright red face. However, I had not bargained for a very mischievous bar man, who at the critical moment when I was making my "maiden speech" on the microphone, "Ladies and Gentlemen it is now..." took great delight in shoving a soaking wet mop up the back of my legs. So my first dignified announcement ended up being, "Ladies and Gentlemen it is now waaaaaaaaaaaahhhhhhh" – how cruel! All the staff laughed hysterically and my face was redder than ever. But it did make it a very memorable occasion and it could only get better after that. Little did I know how I would need to be confident speaking into a microphone in the future.

We took part in a training course to help us with communication. This was very important for us, as Managers needed to communicate confidently to the staff and customers. We were trained in a classroom environment and people took it in turns to go across a corridor into another room where a video camera was set up. We all had to go into the room two at a time to interview one another, in front of the video camera, with the full class watching and criticising in the room across the corridor. The idea was to see how many times you scratched your head, said "mmmmm" or displayed any other unhelpful habits during a conversation.

I had no self-confidence and I was crippled with fear but it had to be done. I kept putting it off, until I was the last person left to go in. I was so frightened that in the end I took my jacket off and placed it over the video camera, so that people could only hear me but not see what I was doing. Once again, little did I know that this was preparation for what the Lord had in store for me in the days ahead.

Another thing we learnt was how to train people, to enable them to reach their maximum potential in their jobs. We mastered the art of making our customers feel special and giving them the best experience of customer care. Again, these were skills that would be very useful in the days to come. Who would have thought that before we were Christians, God would be training and preparing us whilst we were managing Berni Inns! No experience is wasted with Jesus as He is always directing us towards our destiny - even when we do not recognise it. He loves us so much and will use every opportunity for our good.

We were promoted several times, moving initially to Chatham, which was a naval port eight miles from Maidstone. The Railway Inn was a lively place where Steve and I worked very hard and learned lots about managing people. A year later, we moved to The Hilden Manor in Tonbridge, a very smart place with lots of challenging staff issues. We uncovered some dreadful situations involving blackmail and theft amongst the staff. We were quickly moved from there and promoted again to be Senior Assistant Managers in a beautiful village steak house called The George which was in Hayes just outside Bromley.

Steve and I poured ourselves into our jobs and as soon as Steve was twenty-one, we were given a license for The Leather Bottle Inn, Edgware. Here we had two bars and a restaurant to manage. We had done very well, as we had become the youngest Berni Inn Steak House Managers in the UK. Life was very tough and we discovered that many of the staff believed it was part of the perks of their job to go home with half of the stock hidden in their bags. Consequently, when we took over The Leather Bottle it was under threat of closure because it was not making a profit.

We started with the challenge of turning it around to make it a success. We had to retrain some staff, sack some staff, recruit and train new ones. We ran incentive schemes and worked very hard almost every day, from 8.30am through to 12.30am, with only a very short rest break in between. The Leather Bottle began to make a good profit and the company decided to redevelop the branch, as it had done so well to recover. This was a good learning curve for us and great preparation for all God had in store for us.

Throughout this time, life for my parents was still as chaotic as ever. The Police would be called out and want to take action, but every time my Mum would back down and refuse to make a complaint against my Dad. This is the usual behaviour for victims of domestic violence, as they cannot bear the burden and guilt of seeing the person they love locked away. They feel condemned and believe it must all be their fault. The victims are generally manipulated and controlled by the person who is supposed to love them. A couple of times things were so bad that we had to drive up overnight to bring Mum back to stay with us for a few days, whilst she recovered from a beating.

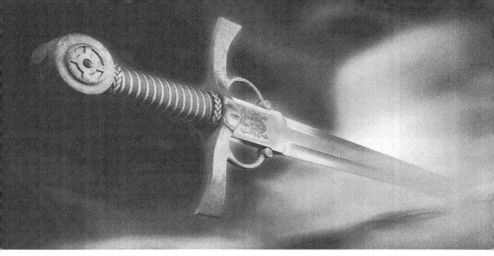

BROKEN & HOMESICK

Steve and I have discussed this next part of our lives together, before I wrote it down and we are in complete agreement in sharing this with you. We do so because we believe that our vulnerability may save you from a violent relationship or save you from losing a relationship that may be saved.

The long hours and intensive lifestyle at Berni Inns satisfied us for a little while. However, the strain of the hard lifestyle, coupled with two people getting married so young and bringing so many unresolved issues into the marriage was not a good combination. For me it was just as though history was repeating itself and I found myself in the midst of a violent relationship. I was desperately unhappy and so was Steve, yet neither of us knew how to handle the stress and the violence.

During one particular row, whilst the Leather Bottle was closed, I found myself running down the stairs terrified, from our flat, through the restaurant, through the bars desperately searching for a safe place to hide. I eventually found my way into the office, where I hid under the desk hoping my breathing was not so loud that Steve could hear it and find me. I could hear Steve stomping around the Leather Bottle shouting after me, furious that I had managed to escape him. It was just like a horror movie only this was my life and it was terrifying! I stayed hidden for quite some time until Steve had calmed down and it was safe to come out again.

Eventually things got so bad that I could not take it any more and I did what I always did and ran. It was the fight or flight reaction and I never wanted to fight - I had experienced enough of that and so I ran. I packed my bags, took a taxi to the railway station and was on the first train back to Liverpool. I did not tell Steve I was going as I was afraid he would stop me.

I arrived back home in Liverpool devastated and unable to face going back to live that life any longer. I loved Steve though and did not want to live my life without him. It did not take long for Steve to track me down and before too long he was on his way back up to Liverpool to see me. Steve and I were heartbroken. However we recognised that we loved each other too much to walk away. We apologised and forgave one another. We were determined that we would do whatever was necessary to restore our relationship. We returned to The Leather Bottle again with the intention of moving back to Liverpool as soon as we could.

A few days later, a rather large lady physically attacked me in the restaurant because she did not like my Liverpool accent. She punched me in the face and I managed to restrain myself from crying in front of her and our staff. But as soon as she was thrown out, I was weeping uncontrollably as my face began to swell and bruise. For me that was the final straw and I was desperate to go back home to Liverpool.

I believe that God creates us with something like a God shaped hole in our lives that Jesus alone can fill. We often try lots of things to fill that hole and sometimes it works but only temporarily. After a year of managing the Leather Bottle, I was very home sick and deeply depressed, it just was not enough anymore. One day I desperately cried out to "this God" that my friend Linda had told me about whilst I was at College some years earlier.

I asked Him if He was real to prove Himself by:

1. Enabling Steve and I to return to Liverpool.
2. Enabling us to have "normal" jobs!
3. Enabling us to have our own home (as we lived in the Leather Bottle).
4. Enabling Steve and I to have a baby; I was desperate for a baby by this time.
5. Enabling us to have a dog.

I pledged that if "this God" who Linda believed in, answered my prayer, I would believe in Him. Now what I did not realise is that God likes a challenge and was in the process of drawing us close to Him.

Within two weeks we were moving back home to Liverpool - prayer 1 answered. We were offered several jobs after simple phone call interviews - prayer 2 answered. We had nowhere to live and once again lived in a single bed in the box room of our parents. My Mum's dog gave birth to a litter of beautiful Springer Spaniel puppies and I had to act as a doggie midwife as she got into a little difficulty delivering them. The final puppy was born right into my hand. God had answered prayer 5 and He could not have done it any more wonderfully.

We had no money and had to sell our car to pay for the deposit on our first real home - prayer 3 answered. That was not a problem, until Steve was offered a job working for an insurance company where he needed a car. However a problem to us was no problem to God as He continued to draw us to Himself. We searched and searched for a suitable car to buy with very little money. Having searched all the garages with no joy, we visited Bill Sanders who had advertised a car in the local newspaper. Bill sold us a rather old but very beautiful red Triumph Dolomite at a price we could afford. What we had not realised was that the Lord had set us up with the Reverend Bill Sanders who made a point of always praying for the people who came across his path. We went away thrilled with our purchase, although we had no idea of the significance of our new car.

After a few months in our lovely home, we were excited to discover I was pregnant after many months of trying - prayer 4 answered. When I was seven months pregnant, we awoke one Sunday morning with a desire to go to church. Sadly, it was not a good experience and we decided never to go again!

I had forgotten my commitment to God. Having answered all my prayers, God was not going to be put off that easily. The next weekend we visited Linda who recognised our lovely Triumph Dolomite car as belonging to Bill Sanders. Bill was a Church of England Curate in a church in Netherton, that Linda's family attended. Linda boldly encouraged us to try this church and to give God another chance. I am sure this was the first sign of hope that Linda had as she prayed for us so faithfully for years. I hope this will encourage you not to give up as you pray for family members, or friends who show no signs of encountering Jesus - they will come through in God's time.

The next weekend, we visited this church and received a very warm and friendly welcome from Bill and all of Linda's family. We went along each week and Sandra (Linda's sister) and her husband Bobby invited us to join their House Group where we experienced much of the presence of God. The members of the House Group were lovely and it is wonderful to look back on that group and know that everyone there are still walking with Jesus. This group moved powerfully in the Gifts of the Holy Spirit and we witnessed many amazing things. To be honest, at the time I thought it was all very weird but I could not keep away.

A few weeks later, I gave birth to our first child after many, many hours of a very painful and difficult labour. I was very ill during the delivery and spent much of the time unconscious. As soon as our son was born, Steve ran out of the hospital and drove straight to the church to give his life to Jesus. Steve was so overwhelmed by the wonder of his son's arrival into the world that he left me unconscious and ran straight into Jesus' arms. I have forgiven him for leaving me there with his newborn son!

For me though the process was not so easy – I had a husband and now a beautiful baby, and this God wanted first place in my life. How could I put God before my husband and little baby son?

I was concerned because all the Christians I had ever met appeared to read their Bibles every day and for me that was a bit of a problem as I hated reading. For some reason I am not aware of, I did not start reading until I was seven years old and I had moved school. Even at that age I was ashamed and embarrassed, and so I cheated. I pretended I could read and desperately tried to catch up to the standard of the other children. So for me reading is still not a joyous activity and as a result I am much more of a "doing person" and find sitting still to read very difficult. It all sounds rather silly, but the difficulty was very real to me and I knew becoming a Christian was a big decision that I wanted to get right.

Several weeks went by and people around me were encouraging me to become a Christian. To be honest I felt under a lot of pressure from them, so on Easter Sunday I made a decision to pray a prayer giving my life to Jesus. This is what I prayed:

"Dear Father God I come to you in the name of Jesus. I acknowledge that I am a sinner, and I am sorry for my sins and the life that I have lived; I need your forgiveness. I believe that your Son Jesus Christ shed His precious blood on the cross and died for me, and I am now willing to turn from my sin. You said that if we confess Jesus as our Saviour and believe in our hearts that God raised Jesus from the dead, we would be saved. I confess Jesus as my Lord. I believe that God raised Jesus from the dead and I accept Jesus Christ as my own Saviour. Thank you Jesus for dying for me and giving me eternal life. Amen."

I do not know what other people experience at these times - I have heard many diverse stories - but I expected to see fireworks and to hear God's voice declaring His pleasure in my decision. Everyone at church was very excited at my announcement. However I have to say personally for me, it was a real disappointment. It appeared that nothing happened, nothing changed. My Dad never wanted me and neither, it appeared, did God.

Was the lack of response from God due to Him not wanting me, or was it due to the fact that I had really prayed to please the people around me and not because I genuinely wanted to become a Christian?

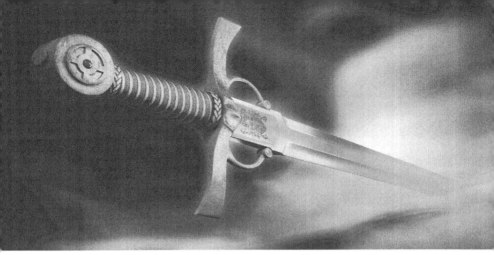

SHATTERING BLOWS

As I share this part of my story, to protect the people involved, I have changed their names. Not long after our son was born, my Dad revealed to us that he had been having an affair for a while. Dad had met Mary through Alcoholics Anonymous (AA) and she had become pregnant! She was a mature lady and had thought she was in the menopause and unable to conceive.

Over my parents' kitchen table, Mary and my Dad discussed the situation together with other members of AA, whilst my Mum was left sitting in another room broken hearted. Mary decided she would not tell her husband, even though it was acknowledged my Dad was the father of the child. Dad was not happy about this decision and my Mum was certainly not happy.

Mary then walked out of our lives and we later heard that she had given birth to a son. It was very strange to know that now I had a half brother, a little younger than my own son! I did not think our paths would ever cross again, however the sins of my Dad and Mary came back to haunt us and caused great pain for many more years to come.

This was a very painful time for our family and for my Mum it was the end of a very traumatic marriage. My Mum began a really difficult, agonising and bitter divorce, which in the end did not bring the freedom or life that either of my parents desired.

When the divorce and settlement were finally approved, they were faced with selling the house. However as they continued to live in the house (although separate lives) the terrible atmosphere caused every prospective buyer to leave and never come back again.

During this time Steve lost his job as an Insurance Agent and we were left with no money at all. I remember walking into the unemployment office, knowing that we had nothing for food and a small child to feed. The staff were unsympathetic, very impatient and unfriendly as I begged them for help. This had to be one of the most degrading moments of my life, as I told them that I was not going to leave until they had done something to help us. Eventually, after much persuasion, they gave us an advance on our benefit and I was able to get some food to cover us for a few days.

This was the first time we really saw God's provision. The Lord was good - often when we were most desperate a bag of groceries would arrive. Thank you Father God! Thankfully Steve soon got a new job as a Taxi Driver.

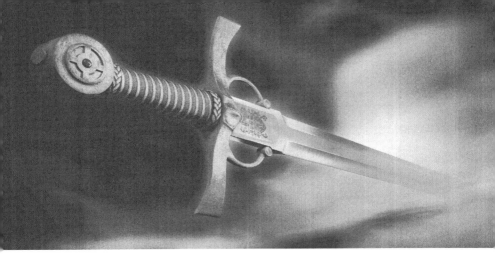

RECEIVING THE SWORD

Steve and I went along to church each week, however personally I was becoming increasingly frustrated, but did not understand why. You see I had signed up for "Acts 2 Christianity" that demonstrates the biblical signs, wonders and miracles that Jesus said we would all be able to do (read it for yourself to be encouraged). I did not become a Christian to fill a pew or to just get my ticket to heaven. I signed up for a relationship with the living God, for salvation and so much more. It is sad to say that at that time we did not see many signs, wonders or miracles, hence the frustration.

Life was really tough and finally, one night, whilst Steve was working and our baby was fast asleep in his cot, I began to vent my frustration on God. I was very depressed and weepy. I felt that I could not go on living like this as our finances were in a terrible state. I had lost all hope for the future and religion was simply not enough. I cried out to God, "Where are You Lord? I know Satan is attacking my life in so many ways, but where are you? You are supposed to be my heavenly Father and I am supposed to hear you speaking to me. I might as well have a relationship with a brick wall and I feel as though I am going to church for a history lesson that is 2,000 years old!"

I really was desperate and I ranted and raved at God, but then He is big enough to take it and actually He longs for us to be real with Him. God does not want us to speak to Him with flowery religious language, especially when we are angry, hurting or frustrated on the inside. God longs for us to be real with Him, so that He can be real with us after all He knows all about it any way.

I had no idea what to expect, but I was desperate and I mean really desperate. Eventually I sobbed myself to sleep. However in the middle of the night I had an incredible encounter with God that has remained with me every minute of every day since then and yet is so difficult to fully explain. I will try to relate it to you. In doing so I must say that at the time I was not very familiar with Scripture and therefore could not have made this up or imagined it.

Suddenly, God appeared and I was positioned on His right side as though He was standing shoulder to shoulder with me. There was an overwhelming and amazing presence displayed by a magnificent, brilliant light, certainly not a natural light. There was an awesome love, an incredible sense of security and peace beyond words. In front of me about three yards away was Satan. I was not scared of him because God was standing with me. Can you believe that? The holy, awesome and magnificent God standing with me, a broken, rejected and hopeless individual! He did not wait for me to be perfect; He came to me when I needed Him most.

God placed a huge double-edged sword into my hands. The sword looked like it was made of shining, gleaming steel without a mark or fingerprint upon it. It was very heavy and very sharp. The sword's handle fitted perfectly into my hand. As I took hold of it, the tip was touching the floor. It was just the right length for me to use. It was as though the sword was made to measure, just for me, and although the Lord gave me no instructions, I automatically knew what to do with it.

For the Lord takes delight in his people; He crowns the humble with victory. Let His faithful people rejoice in this honour and sing for joy on their beds. May the praise of God be in their mouths and a double-edged sword in their hands. Psalm 149:4-6

Knowing God was standing with me, I fixed my gaze upon Satan. Using all my strength, I took the sword in both hands, raising it from the floor until the tip was facing Satan. Without me speaking or taking any further action, the simple movement of raising the double-edged sword into position, caused Satan to flee immediately.

Deuteronomy 33:29 tells us that God is our shield and helper and our glorious sword. Our enemies will cower before us.

The Lord filled me with His presence, His awesome, amazing, powerful and overwhelming peace. He then spoke to me and said "I will never leave you or forsake you and I will always be there for you".

This encounter with the Lord completely changed me from being hopeless, depressed and weepy - to being filled with hope, new life and unspeakable joy. I did not realise it but I had also been baptised, or some say filled, with the Holy Spirit. The following day was as though everything was brighter and more beautiful and I was seeing life through a new pair of eyes.

I had discovered that God was real and nobody could ever take that away from me. I had longed to encounter God, to hear His voice, to know His presence and to understand how much He loved me. God met with me and I had never encountered such overwhelming love and it completely changed my life forever.

As the years have unfolded since that event I have come to understand the implications of what happened. The Lord had put a double-edged sword in my hand and He has been teaching me how to use it ever since. I know that

God revealed Himself to me in that way because He knew what was ahead of me!

I encourage you, if you have never had an encounter with God or received the baptism of the Holy Spirit, to cry out to God and ask Him to meet with you. He loves you so much and He longs for you to come into His presence. Please never settle for just a religious experience - press into God for an intimate relationship, as without that we will never encounter the fullness of God. As Christians, it is essential for us to be filled with the Holy Spirit - without Him we are powerless. The Holy Spirit opens the word of God up to us and gives us revelation and understanding. The Holy Spirit provides the gifts we need to empower us and enables us to be the church that will disciple the nations.

The Holy Spirit displays God's power through each of us as a means of helping the entire church. To one person the Spirit gives the ability to give wise advice; someone else may be especially good at studying and teaching, and this is his gift from the same Spirit. He gives special faith to another, and to someone else the power to heal the sick. He gives power for doing miracles to some, and to others power to prophecy and preach. He gives someone else the power to know whether evil spirits are speaking through those who claim to be giving God's messages - or whether it is really the Spirit of God who is speaking. Still another person is able to speak in languages he never learned; and others, who do not know the language either, are given power to understand what he is saying. It is the same and only Holy Spirit who gives all these gifts and powers, deciding which each one of us should have. 1 Corinthians 12:7-11 (The Living Bible)

SEARCHING FOR THE SPIRIT OF GOD

Several months after I received the sword from the Lord, Steve and I moved from the Netherton church with no clear idea where we were moving to. I had become a Christian anticipating an Acts 2 walk with God (signs, wonders and miracles) and that was not happening where we were. We were hungry for more of God and we did not know where we would find that in a church. We looked for a church that welcomed children, where our little son would be loved and welcomed too. We visited several churches including a house church in the Waterloo district of Liverpool that had recently moved into their own building. We settled in well and grew in the midst of this lively church that encouraged people to be operating in the gifts of the Holy Spirit.

Gradually I began to think I might be hearing God speaking to me, but I was not sure. Maybe it was just me or maybe it was Satan. It is easy be confused until you learn to recognise God's voice. This was not an audible voice, but a voice in my head encouraging me to go and visit a lady who had recently been diagnosed with cancer, so I offer to pray for her to be healed. However, immediately another voice was saying to me that she would just think I was stupid and if she was not healed what would she think then? I battled between these two voices and sadly took no action.

Some time later a wonderful American prophet, Dennis DeGrasse, visited our church. Dennis prayed for me and said, "God wants you to know that the voice you have been hearing has been the voice of the Lord and He wants you to learn to recognise His voice."

Now it is usually easy to judge between those two voices; God's voice is mostly the one that is speaking life, whilst the other voice speaking negatively is usually Satan.

We learn to recognise God's voice by spending time with Him. Just as I spend time with my husband Steve and I know how to recognise his voice. Steve now works on an oil and gas platform in Liverpool Bay and is away from home for two weeks at a time. When Steve is away and he rings me, he does not need to introduce himself to me. He does not need to say his name or where he lives - I recognise his voice and the way he speaks to me. Learning to recognise the way that God speaks to you is just the same. Sometimes God's voice can sound just like your voice or He may speak to you through the scriptures, or a picture, or a dream. God is the creator and He speaks to us through so many different sources and it is really important that you learn to recognise how He speaks to you. After all without recognising God's voice how do we know what we should be doing with our lives?

It is important to understand who you are and what the gifts are that God has made available for you. So often many Christians never discover who God has destined them to be and never receive the gifts that God has made available. Sometimes that is because they never receive the teaching or encouragement to begin to take hold of their gifts or are given a safe place to practise using them. God has chosen you and He has gifts just for you - take hold of them and put them to good use.

I quickly discovered that God has made me to be a visionary and pioneering person, with a heart to see people meet Jesus. I was invited to help lead the Sunday morning group for pre-schoolers and as I prayed about it, the Lord clearly spoke to me. He spoke words that would become the hallmark of my life and ministry in this particular church. The Lord said "Never expect man to thank you for what you are doing. What you do, you do to please me!" So, on that basis I accepted the invitation.

I worked with a wonderful woman of God in leading the work with the pre-school children and their families. We redeveloped the crèche into a really powerful area of ministry and after praying the Lord said it should have a new name, "Kindlers". Kindlers!!!

I have to admit I had no idea what that meant, but looking it up, I was overwhelmed that this was indeed a name chosen by God. Kindlers are small pieces of wood used for starting a fire and spiritual Kindlers was exactly what we believed the Lord wanted our children to be.

Ministering with the children and their families was great fun as we saw many young children filled with the Holy Spirit and praying for each other, releasing miracles in their midst. We also prayed for families and women who were struggling to conceive and we saw God move many times in those areas. Several women declared barren by their doctors conceived the most beautiful babies. Praise the Lord for He is the giver of life!

One precious couple I had prayed for were just about to start IVF treatment when one day I looked at her and the Lord showed me she was pregnant. I asked her if she had anything to tell me, but actually she did not because she did not even know herself. A couple of weeks later she came to see me and said, "How did you know before I did?" She went on to have a beautiful little boy. A gift from God without IVF!

Another lady had one daughter and was desperate for another child. Time had gone on with no joy. I was invited to pray for her and her husband. Within a couple of months they conceived and had a gorgeous baby girl.

Another couple could not conceive and had given up all hope. They had just started the process of adoption when she discovered she was pregnant. They went ahead with the adoption and now they actually have three beautiful daughters. There have been many more babies conceived and born. I am sure too that there are many babies we do not even know about yet.

I was often at the forefront of pioneering and reaching out to those who did not yet know Jesus. One of the works I pioneered was a Puppet Theatre Team. The Lord told us it would be a tool for the hard hearted where no other tool would work.

To begin with, I took on responsibilities of leadership whilst waiting for a man of God to rise up and take the lead. As a woman, I struggled to believe that God could use me and particularly as I did not have a theological degree. That was never said to me by anyone else but it was something I simply believed. We often come under a spiritual influence that affects what we believe and how we live, without even a word being said. Even today, in many churches women cannot minister in senior leadership positions and are encouraged to minister with the children, administration or in the kitchens, etc. It is never openly said, but often women do not have the opportunity to rise into leadership positions.

It took quite some time for the Lord to change my mindsets and position me to operate in all that He had for me as a leader, who happened to be a woman. Please allow Father God to expose any mindsets you may have that hold you back from all that God has destined for you. It does not matter if you are a man or a woman, God has a unique plan for your life and all the gifts to empower you to fulfil that plan if only you will allow Him.

The Lord taught me so much about leading people and how much I could trust Him. One example of this was two elderly ladies who both wanted to be in the Puppet Team but who did not like each other at all - I had to ensure one was put in the front of the theatre whilst the other was in the back! I learnt diplomatic skills with those precious women.

We also had so many times of great fun with our Puppet Team and the characters they played. The Puppets often impacted the lives of those adults who appeared to have the hardest of hearts. When we were out with them, we would frequently see crowds of grown men watching our performances. We saw many people of all ages introduced to Jesus through the work of the Puppet Theatre. The great news is we also saw lots of miracles. One wonderful example happened in Halifax. At the end of our ministry with Greedy Gus, Sindy Sensation, Smart Alec, Shy Anne and Henry Heartthrob (those were the Puppets' names!) we offered to pray for people who needed healing. Several people responded including a couple that were desperate for a miracle.

I was mentoring a young lady and so I took her with me to pray for this couple. Immediately the Lord said, "Tell them they will walk on the mountain tops again!" (This was a word of knowledge - when God tells you something that you do not know about the person who needs the miracle). As I repeated what the Lord had said this precious couple burst into tears. Not the reaction I was expecting!

They recounted their story. Brian had very serious heart and lung problems and was on the Addenbrooke's Hospital's waiting list for a double heart and lung transplant. Before Brian's illness they had loved walking and particularly walking on the tops of the mountains. The young lady at my side went white, but I assured her that in God's eyes there is no difference between a headache and the need for a double organ transplant. We prayed for Brian and his wife and then waited to hear what the Lord had done.

The good news is that when you get a word of knowledge, it often means that God is going to heal that person. We heard a few months later that Brian's lungs had been healed completely and he was then fit enough for them to operate on his heart. Why did God not heal Brian's heart too; I've no idea!

The same weekend a young man who had been born blind was healed and his sight was restored. Our God is amazing!

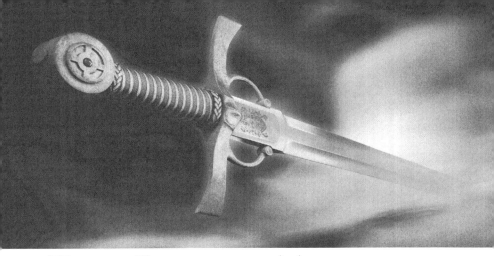

THE GOD OF MIRACLES

We moved to a lovely terraced house. Our little boy was so thrilled to be able to have a little garden to play in. Our precious dog was a great companion for him and they adored each other. Soon after we moved home and church, Steve and I got baptised in water together. This was a very powerful time for us. What we did not know at the time was that I was pregnant again.

A little way into the pregnancy I began to bleed and there was some concern that I may lose the baby. Following a scan, we discovered that I had eight problems with the pregnancy including placenta previa, which meant that if the pregnancy managed to come to full term, I would need to have a Caesarean section. The pregnancy was very difficult with so many problems but I knew my God was able to heal and to save. When I was around seven months' pregnant, a couple of the church elders visited us at home to pray for us and almost immediately seven of the pregnancy problems were overturned. That's my God - He is our healer and deliverer!

I reached full term and was admitted into hospital with yet another problem. The consultant, Mr Abdulla, was a really sweet man and after reading my notes decided to start the delivery of my baby. I quickly went into labour and our daughter arrived before any of us were ready. In fact she was born so quickly I did not make it into the delivery room and she was here before the pain relieving drugs had time to kick in. I made a sound that nobody could ignore!

Our daughter was beautiful and I was in awe as I had missed out in the joy of holding our son when he was born. Our little girl was a miracle baby, a baby who may never have been born had God not answered our prayers. God is so good at miracles.

JEHOVAH JIREH - OUR PROVIDER

Steve and I suffered yet another financial crash. Steve was still a taxi driver and the car was forever going wrong. This meant that not only did he incur huge vehicle repair bills, but also he lost a lot of money whilst the car was off the road being repaired. It always seemed to go wrong at the weekends when the maximum amount of earnings could be made.

After the birth of both our children, I suffered terrible post-natal depression. Thankfully, a sympathetic doctor quickly recognised the symptoms and provided the help I needed.

Steve in his naive sweetness, trying to take some of the pressure off me, was looking after all our finances. He was struggling to keep up the mortgage payments and, trying to protect me, he had been hiding the letters from our mortgage lender. He had been waiting until he had saved the full amount before paying our mortgage debt but something always cropped up and delayed the payment.

Believe me this is NOT the way to deal with debt problems. Burying your head in the sand just increases the problems. If you find yourself having financial difficulties never ignore them, go and get some help as soon as possible.

One day whilst Steve was out, some post arrived addressed to us both instructing us to appear in court the following day. The mortgage company, believing they were not going to be paid at all, had taken steps to begin the process of repossessing our home. As you can imagine, I was shocked and devastated. I immediately rang the mortgage company but it was too late to prevent us from having to attend court.

I prayed and prayed. Terrified that we were about to lose our home, we attended court. However, Steve had brought with him the money he had managed to accrue and we immediately paid that towards the debt. The mortgage company kindly renegotiated our payments and we gratefully returned with the keys to our home still in our hands. The Lord taught us both so much as we learnt not to hide our problems away. We began the process of selling anything of value we possessed to survive and get through this difficult financial time. I sold any remnants of jewellery I owned, clothing and furniture; anything to keep food on the table and a roof over our head for our children.

Again and again we saw God's miraculous provision. One day it was somebody's birthday and I only had £5 with nothing in the bank to fall back on. The Lord said I was to spend the £5 to purchase a simple birthday gift. In obedience I did exactly that, not knowing how God would provide. As I returned from presenting this small gift, I discovered a white envelope stuck under our front door. There was no name on it and no indication of what I would find inside. My fingers were shaking as I tore open the envelope and with awe and amazement I discovered a £20 gift from Father God! Often, just when we needed it, there would be another envelope containing exactly what we needed.

BACK TO WORK

When our daughter was 6 months old, I had to return to work because of our financial state. Returning to work broke my heart, as I did not want to leave my babies. However, I managed to get a job working part time for Liverpool City Council's Architects Department. I thank God for this job as we had a small Christian Fellowship for the staff made up of personnel from across the city and it was my first experience of the wider church.

It was as we met in the beautiful Liverpool Town Hall to pray that we noticed a new tourist leaflet informing people of all the attributes of this amazing building. One attribute we did not find so amazing was the ten feet high Minerva that was positioned on the top of the dome over the Town Hall. The leaflet quoted that Minerva, the so-called "goddess of wisdom", was the one to whom the residents and businesses of Liverpool attributed their success. What rubbish! Something rose up inside of me and I could not let that one go by unchallenged! I did not realise that God was going to teach me so much and was about to release me into another realm of ministry.

After praying, we wrote a polite letter to the City Council challenging the statement in the leaflet and requesting its removal as soon as possible. We received a very positive response and the leaflet was removed from circulation. We believed that God heard the cries of our heart and any demonic powers that had operated over our city through Minerva were locked up and negated.

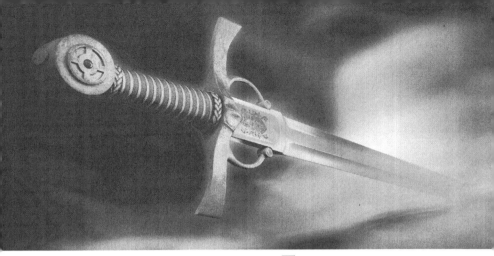

FACE TO FACE

God blessed us through someone providing a holiday for us in a Christian holiday park. Each evening there would be a time of worship and a speaker. The guest speaker did not like Liverpool or people from Liverpool. He was constantly making "nasty jokes" against the people from Liverpool. I tried to smile along but as it continued I felt as if I was being bullied. I felt angry and struggled to deal with how I was feeling. I chose to release forgiveness and to bless this man. Nevertheless I had reached a point where I could not bare to listen any longer.

One evening I was under the impression that the youth team were about to speak in the meeting. However, soon after the start of the meeting they all filed out, inviting the young people to follow them downstairs. Oh no! I had passed the stage of qualifying as a young person and I was not happy. I really didn't want to listen to this man speaking again!

A lovely young man began to lead some simple praise and worship. He did not have the best voice but he had a strong anointing. It is essential we do not miss out on all that God wants to do because like the style or the particular sound is not to our liking. The Bible tells us God's anointing breaks the yoke - something was certainly being broken off my life that night.

As I pressed into God I suddenly found myself in a totally different environment. I was no longer in the meeting hall surrounded by lots of other people. I was in this amazingly spectacular environment standing before the Lord. It was very bright and very beautiful but I felt so unworthy and so filthy dirty. I stood before the Lord and wept, tears streaming down my face. How could this holy, awesome, majestic God even allow me to stand in His presence? He does so because He IS a loving merciful God, who loves to meet with us, to wash us, to cleanse us and to set us apart for His purposes. I was completely overwhelmed by the love of God and His compassion for me. Without speaking to me, the Lord filled me with His peace and totally encompassed my very being inside and out.

I felt as though I had been away from the meeting for such a long time and yet only a few minutes had gone by. I looked around the room bewildered, to find myself standing alongside Steve again, with tears still streaming down my face. I felt so full of peace and a deep, deep sense of God's love for me.

At the end of the meeting, I spoke to the couple hosting the evening and asked them to pray for me. They believed the Lord was setting me apart and He was preparing me for a very powerful ministry in the days ahead. Me? Really? I still struggled to believe that God would want to use me in that way but I could not deny what had happened to me. The Bible tells us in the Psalm 18:35 (BNIV) that God stoops down to make us great; to make us great! Can you believe that? God stoops down to make you great! So let's make the most of that.

God chose the foolish things of the world to shame the wise; God chose the weak things of the world to shame the strong. 1 Corinthians 1:27

This scripture is such an encouragement to me, as I am overqualified to be chosen by God. If God can use me, He can use anyone and, if you do not mind me saying, that includes you!

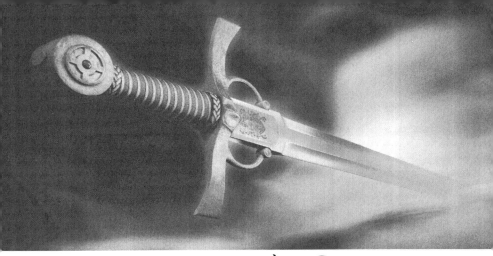

INTO GOD'S CARE

My Dad's behaviour was still very erratic and he was also very vulnerable. Whilst praying one day the Lord told me to go and pray for him and put him into God's care. How scary was that as Dad was still horrible to me! I visited him and to my delight he allowed me to pray for him. I prayed a simple prayer, placing Dad into God's care. With hindsight I was so glad that I overcame my fears and obeyed what God had said.

Within a few weeks my Dad went on a drinking binge. He was very drunk and then on top of that consumed a bottle of 200 Paracetamol tablets and several packs of Co-dydramol painkillers in an attempt to end his life. (This was when you could still buy such large quantities, but because of the number of suicides, the amount has been reduced dramatically). Dad went to bed hoping and expecting to go to sleep and never wake up again.

However, God had other ideas. To his disappointment, Dad regained consciousness thirty six hours later, angry that he was still alive. I did not discover what he had done until after he woke up. When I told Dad's doctor what he had done, he said he had swallowed enough tablets and drank enough alcohol to kill a bull elephant! Dad's survival was a powerful miracle!

I visited my Dad and told him not to try that again. I reminded him that I had put him into God's care and that is where he would stay until God was good and ready to take him. He never attempted to take his life again after that! If God speaks to you as He did to me, please do not ignore His instructions - my obedience enabled the Lord to save my Dad's life.

After further traumas with my Dad, I desperately prayed a dangerous prayer. I asked God to do whatever was necessary to help my Dad to become a Christian. Whilst I am certain that God does not inflict illness and disease, I know that God can move mightily in the midst of it, if we allow Him to. One of those situations arose when a little while later Dad was unwell.

Dad was never very confident and could not remember what was said to him or the questions he should be asking. So when he had to go to hospital for tests, I went along with him. He was grateful for my help, particularly as we discovered that he had a cancerous tumour in his oesophagus. The doctors were worried about telling him because of his mental state, but shortly before Christmas, Dad was advised that he needed radical surgery that would result in the removal of his stomach, oesophagus, spleen and part of his pancreas immediately in the New Year.

My Dad was dismayed and frightened and I could empathise with him as I had faced serious surgery only a few years earlier myself. My surgery had forced me to face the "what ifs?" and I had faced the prospect of not waking up or recovering from my surgery. I had faced it knowing that if anything happened to me Jesus would welcome me lovingly into His arms and that He had prepared a place for me. I went into my surgery confident and in complete peace and thankfully came out and made a full recovery.

So just before Christmas, Dad and I walked into one of our favourite places, the Liverpool Anglican Cathedral. We were both very emotional as I gently talked to Dad and explained that he might survive this surgery to live for many more years or his time may be short. We did not know what the future held except that one day we would all face death. However, we needed to face death confidently, knowing that we are going to meet with Jesus face to face and be received by the Father into heaven or there is no hope.

We must also face life knowing that God alone numbers our days. We need to make the most of every one, whether there are just a few days or many years. It is important to know God's timing for people and this was God's time for my Dad. There in the Cathedral I was privileged to introduce my Dad to Jesus. Gone was the burden of his sinful and angry past and he was filled with the loving acceptance of Father God. He changed dramatically from this man who longed to die, to a man who was looking death in the eye. He now wanted to live and to make the most of what time he had left, however long that would be. This man, who had been the biggest pain and cause of trauma in my life, lived the rest of his days doing his best to bring reconciliation to all he had previously hurt.

The day after Dad's surgery was his 57th birthday. It was not quite springtime but I hunted high and low to find daffodils for him, as they were his favourite flower and a real sign of hope.

GRIPPED BY FEAR

I had passed my driving test first time many years earlier, but somehow fear had gripped my heart and I never drove. In fact travelling anywhere outside of Liverpool, used to grip me with terror to the point where I was almost physically sick. Travelling up and down to the hospital on public transport was difficult and I was fearful that if something happened to my Dad I would not get there in time. I decided that it was time for me to take God at his word and to repent of the fear and trust God to give me the courage to drive again. Sounds easy, but fear gripped my heart like a strong vice and I cried out to God to empty the very busy local dual carriageway until my confidence was restored. God is so kind as literally every time I approached the dual carriageway it was like the parting of the Red Sea, and

God would hold back all the lorries until I had completed my journey. Slowly my confidence grew and I was able to travel around Merseyside without panic and terror gripping my heart and stomach. God wants us to be free of fear and if fear is gripping your life, I recommend you allow God to help you to overcome it.

Dad made a good recovery and initially came out of hospital to stay with my family. I was working part-time and so it was easier for me to care for Dad at my home. It was a very difficult time as my parents were divorced and because my brother lived in Surrey he was not able to help or support very much because of his work commitments.

Some of Dad's brothers and sisters came to see him. They were a broken family; broken by their past and broken by their present. To give you a tragic snap shot - many of their children (my cousins) have been involved in prostitution, drugs and violent crime. Dad had not been out of hospital very long when one of those cousins was sentenced to twelve years in prison for importing and distributing illegal drugs. Another cousin had his two children taken into care because they were born addicted to heroin as a result of their parents' addiction. One cousin was a real beauty in her early years but had turned to prostitution to fund her heavy drugs habit.

Another married a bully and a heavy drinker. One day whilst she was out and her husband was minding their children, their little boy, just a toddler, ran out into the road in front of a lorry and was killed. This was a desperate and heartbreaking tragedy which should never have happened. Another cousin around that time strangled his wife to death during an argument in their home. A few months later, another cousin was arrested and later found guilty of murdering a nightclub doorman. A broken family indeed! Dad never said very much about them; they were his family after all.

I am constantly amazed that Jesus chose to set me apart otherwise I have no idea what my life may have been like. Despite the most difficult of days,

I was able to keep going because I kept my eyes on Jesus. He had promised that He would never leave or forsake me and He never did.

Although it was practically difficult having Dad living with us, it was a precious time for us as he seemed to go from strength to strength. A few weeks later, one beautiful sunny spring morning, Dad and I went out together into Liverpool. We had a lovely time and the day appeared to be overflowing with hope for the future. He seemed so well and full of life but we did not know of the terror that was lurking.

During the night Dad woke me. He had a very high temperature and had been coughing up blood. I rang for a doctor to no avail, so I called an ambulance having no idea of how very ill Dad was.

The ambulance arrived and the staff were so gentle and reassuring as I travelled in the ambulance with my Dad. I had rung my Mum and she followed the ambulance in her car. Dad was whisked through and the doctors began to care for him straight away. I still had no idea of how very ill he was.

A few minutes later the doctor took me, as Dad's next of kin, into a room to tell me that Dad was very poorly with pneumonia and they were expecting that he would stop breathing. They knew from their records that he had cancer and suddenly I found myself being asked what I would want them to do if he stopped breathing. How could I determine whether my Dad should live or die, whether they should try to resuscitate him or leave him to pass away? Was that even legal? I was completely bewildered and certainly did not want the responsibility of deciding whether my Dad should live or die.

I tried to speak to my brother but the telephone simply kept ringing out. In the end I called the Police and they had to drive around to knock my brother out of bed and get him to call me at the hospital. Once again I felt like I had the weight of the world upon my shoulders. The pressure and the responsibility were crushing. While I was waiting for my brother and his wife to complete their four hour drive, I rang the Pastor of our church who kindly prayed with me that God would take the decision out of my hands. God is so good and as we prayed Dad miraculously recovered.

Dad enjoyed a few more months and made the most of every day. Then one day he had gone over to Manchester to stay at one of his brothers when he rang to say that he was not feeling very well. He returned home and after a visit to the doctors and a scan a few days later, we were told that the cancer was now in his liver. We made the most of those last few weeks and there was great reassurance to see the reality of Dad's salvation as he faced death with great courage, confidence and peace.

The Marie Curie welcomed Dad at their hospice in Woolton, Liverpool and just a few days before he died, we managed to gather those of his brothers and sister together who were still alive (three had died of cancer already) to throw a little party for them all. The most difficult one to track down was my Uncle Stan who was the oldest of the brothers. He was now a widower after my Auntie Eileen had died many years earlier. He had never recovered from losing his beloved wife whom he adored. He had lost himself in alcohol and was in a dreadful mess when we found him. He was delighted to see my Dad and the rest of his brothers and sisters again. Despite the sadness of Dad's deteriorating health it was a time of great joy and laughter as they reminisced and retold stories of their childhood together. Dad went to be with Jesus full of peace, grace and dignity. I thank God for the Marie Curie Hospice who provided the most beautiful care and ensured that Dad did not suffer unnecessarily.

Looking back things can be so funny to reflect on and the day of taking my Dad's ashes to be scattered was one of those days. I collected the ashes from the undertakers whilst two of my Uncles waited at my Mum's house. They wanted to be there as we took Dad's ashes to his favourite place in Great Crosby village. The Undertaker was very slow in releasing the ashes to me, resulting in me being half an hour late driving to my Mum's. In my panic I was driving quickly towards Mum's house when I spotted a police officer standing in the middle of the road. She pulled me over and my immediate thought was that something had happened and they needed my help; Well, that is what you think isn't it? I pulled my car over to ask how I could help them. I imagined that someone had collapsed or that there was some major emergency that required MY help! Super Sue to the rescue - that was who I thought I had to be, always there to sort everyone's problems out!

The Police Officer asked me to step out of my car whilst they asked if I had realised what speed I had been driving. I saw the funny side of the situation and just burst out into hysterical laughter. Not good and certainly not helpful when you are pulled over for speeding. Instead of emotionally explaining that I had my Dad in the boot of my car (well his ashes) I laughed hysterically! This did not bring forth empathy or sympathy from the Police Officer and instead I found myself being booked for my first and only driving offence.

I was very nervous about what I should do with the ashes and being booked by the police a few minutes earlier did not help. I arrived at my Mum's house to be greeted by frowns on all their faces. They were not amused that they had been kept waiting. We drove to Dad's favourite beauty spot and took the lid off the pot ready to scatter the ashes. However, it was a very windy day and as we tried to scatter the ashes they ended up all over our shoes; not very holy or reverent. I do think my Dad would have seen the funny side of it!

We tracked Uncle Stan down once again and it was very clear that he had not been coping on his own. He had serious mental health issues, probably brought on by his severe drinking problem. His sight was very poor and his hygiene was in desperate need of some assistance. My heart was breaking for him and I could not bear to see him being left as he was. The house was filthy and freezing and it was clear that he had not been paying his bills, as there was a mountain of red letters from the suppliers ready to cut off his gas and electric supplies.

With help from Social Services we arranged for Uncle Stan to be taken into Angora Bank Residential Home nearby for respite. It was decided that if he settled in well, they would give Uncle Stan the option of staying and, if he chose to do this, his home would be sold to cover the costs of his care. Uncle Stan was checked over and had some surgery for cataracts in both eyes that certainly helped his quality of life dramatically.

It was decided that he would stay at the Home. A few weeks later Mum and I took him back to his house to pick up any possessions he wanted to keep before the house was emptied and sold. As we arrived at the house I was alarmed to find the front door was open. I was afraid that the house had been burgled or that someone was currently in the house. I found a neighbour who was willing to come in with us just in case anyone was there who should not be. To my absolute horror, I discovered my Uncle Stan's brother and sister ransacking it. They had filled bags and boxes full of his possessions. I decided to give them the benefit of the doubt and hoped against hope that they were planning to take it around to Uncle Stan at his home in Angora Bank. I watched as they filled the boot of the car with lots of boxes and bags and then they followed us back to the home. They had never visited him there before but there is always a first time.

They came into the residential home with us and Uncle Stan was very excited to see them. However, they did not bring in any of the boxes or bags. In fact it was worse than that, my Uncle took me to one side and threateningly told me to back off from Uncle Stan. I was shocked and appalled. I was praying, asking the Lord what I was to do because Uncle Stan was oblivious and thrilled that his brother and sister had come to see him, and I did not want to spoil that for him. I was willing to stay and challenge what had happened but knew that would distress my Uncle Stan. I felt the Lord release me from any further involvement and I have not seen any of them since.

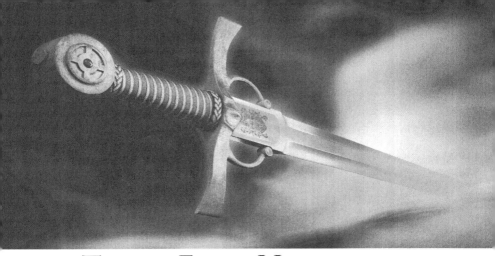

TIME FOR HEALING

This was a devastating season of death. In a period of fifteen months, my Mum's Auntie Dilys and Uncle Ben died within twenty-two hours of each other - which was quite sweet for them as they would never have coped without each other; he always called her the boss and she was! My next-door neighbour and friend Josie died of cancer; a beloved friend Jim who gave you a hug like Father God himself was hugging you, collapsed very suddenly and died three days later of a brain tumour that nobody had known about; a cousin aged 28 died of cancer leaving a wife and two young children; a young and precious man from church died of Leukaemia and then a friend at church's only son died following an accident on his motorbike. A lady from church with a history of severe depression escaped from the psychiatric hospital and threw herself in front of a train. Tragedy after tragedy and there was still more to come.

My Dad and his sister Violet died within six weeks of each other and I think Auntie Violet died of a broken heart after Dad died. We were called when she went into a coma and I felt the Lord was calling me to pray with her. I went along to the hospital knowing that Auntie Violet was in a coma but that she could probably still hear me. I asked God to give me the courage I needed and then stood to my feet to pray for Auntie Violet. I quietly explained how much Jesus loved her and had prepared a place for her. Then I gently prayed a prayer of salvation, encouraging Auntie Violet to respond in her heart. There was no outward sign of a response, but I knew God had sent me there and God would see her response. Within a few hours Auntie Violet too was gone. A season of death indeed and it was not over yet.

During the time leading up to Dad's death I was exhausted. Trying to balance family, work, ministry, and also caring for Dad had also taken it out of me. Shortly before Christmas I clearly heard the Lord. He spoke to me about my exhaustion and said that my life was full of scarred tissue and this prevented Him from using me the way He wanted to. He showed me a picture of a chocolate orange with all its' segments. As you tap the top of the chocolate orange the whole thing falls apart. The Lord said that this is what would happen to me, if He filled me with His power the way He wanted to. I would not be able to contain it and would fall apart. The Lord is a gentleman and asked my permission to heal me - seemed simple enough, so of course I said yes. Little did I know that I was about to experience God's extravagant fire once again!

I continued trying to spin all the plates; family, work and the ministry of the Puppet Theatre until the Lord said I was to lay down the work of the Puppet Theatre so that He could heal me. After our last session before Christmas in the New Strand Shopping Centre, I told the team of my decision to stop. Most of the team took the news very well and they all understood how exhausted I was and how much I needed time to recover.

After Christmas instead of feeling better, the exhaustion grew worse and I began to feel very weepy. I did not feel as if this was because I was grieving for my Dad, as I knew he was with the Lord and I would not have wanted him back to his previous life. I knew He was with Jesus and was celebrating His salvation.

I began to experience flashbacks that were very frightening. A flashback is like a video play back of the most traumatic moments of your past. You do not simply see it; you go through all the emotions and the traumas all over again, and again and again. Flashbacks are very frightening and shattering, both emotionally and physically. You never know when they are going to happen during the day or the night, or what the flashback will be related to, or how long it will last for.

The flashbacks would be about my childhood and the violence that surrounded me. One of the flashbacks that occurred most frequently was of a time when my Dad was really ill and we were driving through the night in the ambulance. I did not understand what was happening to me, and why I was having these flashbacks. I was fearful that I was losing my mind. My sleep patterns were erratic and broken, leaving me completely shattered. In fear and trepidation I visited my doctor expecting the worst.

The doctor was so kind and understanding. She listened intently, as through floods of tears, I explained what I had been experiencing. She explained to me how my body had never had an opportunity to emotionally and physically overcome the traumas that had affected me in the past. It was as though every week whilst Dad was still alive, there was a new problem to overcome and survive. The doctor explained that now my Dad had died, it was as though my body was recognising it was safe to deal with the trauma.

She explained that I was suffering from Post Traumatic Stress Disorder and that it would take some time to recover. She said that often soldiers who had been in very traumatic war situations coped at the time because they had to, but once they returned home, the Post Traumatic Stress hit them when it was safe for their bodies to deal with all that they had faced. She explained that what had happened to me was very similar to that. She suggested I should go for some counselling and that would be organised through the health service and she prescribed some anti-depressants to help me to sleep and to cope in the mean time.

The next nine months were some of the darkest months of my life. I cried so much I could have solved any drought problem all by myself! Psalm 56:8

tells us that God takes our tears and stores them in a bottle; our tears are very precious to the Lord. He must have had a huge bottle for mine!

Do not be afraid of releasing your tears. Do not hold back, as very often they are an important part of your healing and recovery.

Sadly, with any form of depression, the church is often the place where we can be encouraged to "get over it" or to "pull ourselves together". This leaves many people feeling condemned and even more isolated. If we break a bone we have no hesitation in taking someone to the hospital for the broken limb to be plastered up. However, we struggle to understand that sometimes, just like the plaster cast holds everything in place while the bone heals, the medication can provide the support while we heal emotionally and mentally.

I kept reminding myself that God had told me He was going to heal the scarred tissue and that He had a plan for my life. That was the light at the end of the long tunnel that I kept focused on and which kept me going through those dark days and nights.

Death after death, trauma after trauma continued and I found it very difficult to even hold my head up. The grief was completely unbearable and just when I felt it couldn't get any worse - it did.

One day whilst I was working in Southport, a town about fifteen miles away, Steve rang from home. I hardly recognised him as he was so distressed and he was struggling to speak. I do not think I had ever heard Steve so distraught and between sobs he asked me to come home straight away. He did not want to tell me what had happened as he was worried about me having to drive home. However, I needed to know and eventually he told me that a dear friend of ours had died. He did not know what had happened but it did not sound good.

Albie had been the key player within the Puppet Theatre team and was usually so much fun. Steve and I had gone on holiday with him and his family many times. We loved him so much and we were bewildered at the news. His daughter was due to marry in a few weeks' time and she and her future husband were in the final stages of buying our house.

I do not know how I got home that day as my head was in total turmoil. I arrived home and contacted friends to be told that Albie had taken his own life. Everyone was completely devastated. We did not know what to do or who to turn to. We did not know what to say or how to pray. We just cried "oh God!" as no other words would come. Sometimes that is enough - God holds us and carries us when we do not know how to cope or what to say.

This reminds me of the story of footprints written by Carolyn Joyce Carty:[1]

One night a man had a dream. He dreamed he was walking along the beach with the Lord. Across the sky flashed scenes from his life. For each scene he noticed two sets of footprints in the sand one belonging to him, and the other to the Lord. When the last scene of his life flashed before him, he looked back at the footprints in the sand. He noticed that many times along the path of his life there was only one set of footprints. He also noticed that it happened at the very lowest and saddest times in his life. This really bothered him and he questioned the Lord about it: "Lord you said that once I decided to follow you, you'd walk with me all the way. But I have noticed that during the most troublesome times in my life, there is only one set of footprints. I don't understand why when I needed you most you would leave me." The Lord replied: "My son, my precious child, I love you and I would never leave you. During your times of trial and suffering, when you see only one set of footprints, it was then that I carried you."

For me this was one of those times when God certainly carried me. There were so many questions and so few answers. But God! People around asked me "How can you still believe in God?"

My tears have been my food day and night, while they say to me all day long, "Where is your God?" Psalm 42:3

These were days of extravagant fire, when I remembered my visitation with God, the day He met with me and put the sword in my hand. I remembered God talking to me about the plans He had for my life. In the difficult and painful times, we need to recall the times when God has met with us and spoken to us and focus on Him. In the midst of my darkest experiences when I could not walk or function, Jesus came and lovingly carried me through second by second, minute by minute, hour by hour, day by day until I was back into the light.

As I have been writing this book another very precious friend of ours has died. He was one of the last people in the world you would have expected to lose their life to suicide. He was fun, mischievous, gentle and caring. He would go more than the extra mile to help others but his mind snapped with the pressures of life. We all tried very hard to save him from death but at the end of the day we could not save him. Sometimes there is nothing we can do to change events as the people around us have a free will to make choices about their life.

If you are reading this and you feel you are at the end of what you can cope with and are considering taking your life - PLEASE, PLEASE DON'T.

For you are loved more than you can ever imagine, by so many people around you, who perhaps do not make the most of the opportunities to tell you. If you will allow Him to, He will bring you through your pain and trauma and He will bring you into victory. There are many people and organisations around who can help you, if only you will allow them to, for example:

The Samaritans (www.samaritans.org) or MIND (www.mind.org.uk).

During that season of death and funerals, I attended the funeral of a beautiful young lady who died of breast cancer. She had loved Jesus with a passion and we knew as we looked at the coffin that she was not there; she had entered heaven and was enjoying living in the presence of Father God.

Like all the funerals we had recently attended, during the service one person after another came and stood alongside her coffin. Each person told their stories of the laughs and adventures they had together. They each said how very much they had loved her and that life would never be the same without her.

I heard the Lord whisper that He wanted us to let people know how much we love them while they are still alive and we should not wait until it was too late. I have made it my business to do that ever since, to always tell people how precious they are and how much I love them. Sometimes that is just what people desperately need to hear and for them it can be the difference between life and death.

HOLY MEDICINE AND A SURPRISE VISIT

After many months of weeping, our little family were invited to join a group of people from church who were going down to stay in log cabins in Devon for the autumn half term break. We did not know the others very well but by coincidence they were all recovering from horrendous traumas too. God was so gracious to us all and we spent so much of our time giggling, especially the ladies.

One of the staff wanted to be baptised and so we baptised him in the river on 1st November, as you do! It was a bitterly cold day and out of concern for the person baptised (after all we really did not want him to freeze to death) we suggested that we should all meet together early in the evening.

We dined out in the local pub, and as we arrived back at our cabin the children were first to enter the lounge. As they did, they burst into fits of laughter and as each person arrived exactly the same thing happened. The lounge was full of people laughing until they were crying. God had been waiting for us to arrive and as we did, He immeasurably poured out His Holy Spirit upon us.

Do not grieve, for the joy of the Lord is your strength. Nehemiah 8:10

The Lord was lavishly pouring His love upon us, restoring our joy and our strength. It had been a very long time since any of us had really enjoyed a good laugh and it was great medicine. God knew just what we all needed!

After about half an hour of incredible joy the Holy Spirit began to speak to us. People who had never given a prophetic word in their lives were suddenly prophesying. It was an amazing atmosphere full of God's presence, when two of the men began to prophecy over me. I was in the early stages of recovering from Post Traumatic Stress and had not been serving God in any official ministry since I had laid down the work of the Puppet Theatre. I had no self-esteem whatsoever and was certainly not expecting God to speak to me. To my surprise I heard them releasing God's word to me but it was truly unbelievable - God was saying that He was pouring out a governmental anointing into my life and that He was going to take me to the nations. God was going to use me to speak and release His words into the lives of Prime Ministers, Kings and rulers. God was going to use me to change some of the governments and nations of the world.

Later I thought, they have definitely got that one wrong! We returned to Liverpool full of joy and little by little I recovered from the Post Traumatic Stress.

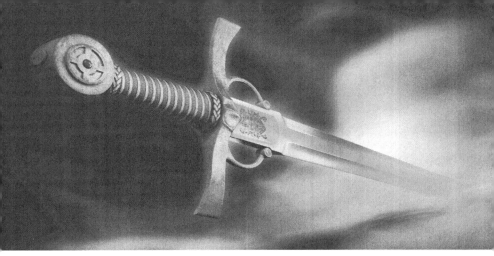

ROOTED

If you read through the scriptures you will see that most people who were used by God, usually paid a high price in order to carry His anointing and power. They went through the Extravagant Fire and came through stronger.

For example, Moses was an outcast and wandered around the desert for forty years before he was used to rescue the children of Israel out of Egyptian slavery. Joseph was wounded, thrown in a pit by his brothers, sold as a slave, falsely accused by his Master's wife and then thrown into jail, before he was used by God to save his nation. Daniel was thrown into the lion's den before he was recognised as a man of God. Ruth was widowed at a young age before she married Boaz. Hannah and Sarah were tortured by barrenness for many years before they conceived children who then went on to change their nations.

It is not that God wants us to suffer; He needs to ensure that we are not just willing, but also really prepared to carry His glory. If we are not prepared, God's power would overwhelm us and we would think it was all abo us and how amazing we are. In the end, that would destroy us and c destroy those around us.

God often allows us to go through these difficult times, even when we have done nothing wrong. The Extravagant Fire burns up all that holds us back and releases the life that has been hidden inside of us. He does that because He has an amazing destiny and plan, not just for our lives, but also for those around us. We need to understand that in our own strength we can do very little, but with God we can do anything He calls us to.

Everything that God calls us to do He empowers us for and releases all the resources to enable us to complete the task. The Lord is looking for those who will love Him enough to invest their lives for the sake of their communities or nations. He is looking for those who will root themselves deeply into God's love and the land around them. When the extravagant fire comes instead of being uprooted and destroyed, those around us watch how we come through the crisis.

When you are rooted into the land you can hear it groaning. During October 2012, Steve and I travelled to New Zealand to stay with our friends, who lived on a hill in Christchurch. They had survived the earthquakes of 2010 and 2011, but they were still living through thousands of aftershocks and tremors. Whilst we were there we experienced several of those shakes for ourselves. It is certainly not a nice experience when you are in the middle of a shower! During the early hours of one night we were awoken by a tremor. Suddenly, Steve and I were wide-awake and alert. A couple of minutes later we heard a loud rumbling coming up the hill, just like a train approaching. The next thing we experienced was a massive shaking as everything in the room around us shook. It was so scary and we later learnt that the tremor had measured 4.8 on the Richter scale. Believe me that was as strong as I wanted to experience! But we had heard the sound of creation really groaning.

I consider that our present sufferings are not worth comparing with the glory that will be revealed in us. For the whole of creation waits in eager expectation for the children of God to be revealed; For the creation was subjected to frustration, not by its own choice, but by the will of the one who subjected it, in hope that the creation itself will be liberated from its bondage to decay and brought into the freedom and glory of the children of God. We know that the whole creation has been groaning as in the pains of childbirth right up to the present time. Not only so, but we ourselves, who have the first fruits of the Spirit, groan inwardly as we wait eagerly for our adoption to sonship, the redemption of our bodies. For in this hope we were saved. Romans 5:18-24

What does this mean? It means that when we become Christians, we are adopted into His family and we can operate as God's representatives here to bring heaven to earth. The problem is that most people do not understand that and therefore never take hold of that authority effectively.

It leaves our communities, towns and cities operating without true authority and the enemy comes in to fill the vacuum. We then see our communities struggling to cope with alcohol, gambling and drug addictions fueling violent crime and abuse. Poverty and cycles of deprivation increase as does poor health and premature death. There is the sound of those who have been enslaved and broken crying out for their lives to change. Have you heard that cry? I certainly have!

We need to live our lives according to God's plan and not come into agreement with the strategies of the enemy. Your life when you have become a Christian can be used to bring the antidote to a broken world. When you see brokenness and deprivation, ask God for the answer. Do not agree with hopelessness and bad news but be a person who causes hope to arise.

As you read and digest the word of God through reading the Bible, you can then declare God's word to bring forth life. You can release life and health where death and sickness has prevailed. You can release resources through prayer, where poverty has crippled individuals, families, communities, cities and nations, businesses, organisations and even governments.

As you have read this book, you will have seen how Jesus accepted me as a completely broken person and transformed me through His love. I would like to share with you some of the things that He has taught me and as I have applied this it has changed my life dramatically.

Jesus has led me step by step until I have been used to mobilise people in prayer and action. This has impacted crime levels, which in turn eased the suffering of families and caused an increased desire for people and businesses to invest into the city.

It's an exciting story, an impossible story, but an extraordinary story, and I hope it will encourage you to be a vessel of change for your sphere of influence.

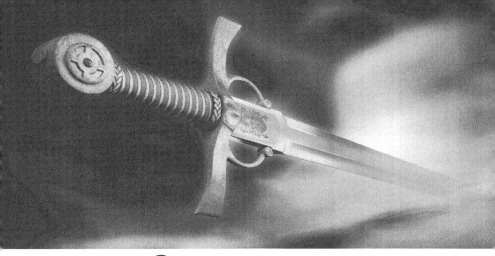

QUESTIONS

In 1997 the Lord challenged me to re-start the Puppet Theatre and I certainly did not want to do that. However, by the time the Lord had spoken to me several times about it, I knew I had no choice. We assembled a team once again but every time we looked at the old puppets and particularly Greedy Gus, they reminded us of Albie.

Last time around, as we visited the local schools Greedy Gus (Albie's puppet) and the other puppets used to get their own fan mail. To show how popular Greedy Gus was here is a little bit of one letter he received from Christopher aged 8: "Im like Greedy Gus I like Mars bars to I have a lot of friends in my class even some of the girls like me its hard to get girls to like you when your a boy they even let me play with them I like them to but they scream a lot after a wile you get a head ake".

I wonder how Christopher is today and if he still makes the girls scream!

We quickly realised that if we were going to start again, then we would need new puppets and new scripts. So we began the process of designing new characters and writing new scripts. Script writing and recording was always great fun.

Last time around we had lots of engagements and people loved the work we did. There were a lot of other great outcomes too, including two weddings of couples that met through volunteering in the team. Simon, a wonderful young man, helped me with the design and construction of the new puppets by carving foam rugby balls into puppet heads. He is now one of the leading chainsaw woodcarvers in the world and has been highly placed in competitions in the USA, Japan, Canada, Holland and the UK.

However, as a Puppet Team we wanted and needed this ministry to be so much more fruitful this time. We were determined that we would spend a lot more time praying, in the hope that we would see more people meeting Jesus, instead of simply watching a puppet show.

We spent Monday evenings practising, which was always hard work physically but full of lots of hysterical laughter, and on Thursday evenings we met to pray.

> When Jesus saw the crowds; he had compassion on them, because they were harassed and helpless, like sheep without a shepherd. Then he said to his disciples, "the harvest is plentiful but the workers are few. Ask the Lord of the harvest, therefore, to send out workers into his harvest field." Matthew 9:36-38

If the harvest was plentiful, why despite our hard work, were we not seeing more people coming to know Jesus as their Saviour?

This was a major training period for me, as the evangelist's frustration within me led me back to the Throne Room of God. I fasted and wept before the Lord, crying out to Father God to show me what the blockage was. It was during one of those times that the Lord led us to go out into our local high street. The Lord told us we were not to pray, nor to give out any evangelistic tracts or get into any conversations. He wanted to show us what He saw there.

We felt like Joshua, Caleb and the other ten spies who were sent out to look at the land of Canaan that the Lord was going to give to them. Interestingly, later in the story (Numbers 14) it says that of all the generation who came out of Egypt, only Joshua and Caleb survived the journey. I know this was a result of the sin of the people, but I do wonder if it was also because they were the only ones who had the vision that God was going to give them the land. They had a sense of purpose that enabled them to survive all that came against them on the journey. A clear vision and purpose are essential for us to survive the difficult days, when all we want to do is give up.

So just like Joshua and Caleb we returned and recorded everything we saw. Then we went out again a couple of nights later, on a dark Monday evening to repeat the process. We returned to the church and once again, recorded all that we saw. We mapped out the number of premises that offered people the opportunity to gamble, to buy or drink alcohol and to buy into things that did not encourage abundant life.

As we looked at the map, the Lord began to reveal to us that there was a Spirit of Death over that area. A Spirit of Death! What is that and what does that mean? Why was God showing us that? How could it be there when God is in control? My mind buzzed with a multitude of questions and no answers. As we fasted and prayed, we knew that God was leading us on a journey of discovery. If we needed any confirmation of the Spirit of Death operating in our community, then we got one only a few days later.

The Waterloo and Crosby area is six miles from the heart of Liverpool and is not usually known for violent crime. For as long as I can remember I do not ever recall any murders there. However just three days later, on 1st October 1998, a man with a gun walked into a small local gym and shot father of four, Kevin McGuire, aged 37, and Nathan Jones, aged 24. One man died at the scene and the other died a little while later at the hospital. The local community was left shocked and very frightened. Someone was soon arrested and after a court case, found guilty of the double murder.

God really had our attention as we wept and cried out to Him to have mercy on us and on our community. We asked the questions, was there something we could have done? Was there something we could have prayed that would have changed the events of that day? We did not know the answers but we needed to learn from what God had been saying and what had happened that terrible day.

It is important to understand that God is the King of Kings and the Lord of Lords; and nothing happens without God's knowledge. If a Spirit of Death was operating in our area, it could not have slipped into our region while God was busy somewhere else or having a sleep! So would it be helpful for us to pray to bind this demonic principality? Would that stop any further death? Questions and more questions!

As I prayed, I believed that the Lord was showing me that just as sin has consequences in our lives, the consequences of sin could also affect our land. A famous scripture that people of prayer use, is 2 Chronicles 7:14-15:

If my people, who are called by my name, will humble themselves and pray and seek my face and turn from their wicked ways, then I will hear from heaven and will forgive their sin and will heal their land. Now my eyes will be open and my ears attentive to the prayers offered in this place.

Just what was holding back the blessing on our region and what was allowing the land to be vulnerable to bad things happening? What were the wicked things that needed to be dealt with? Questions and more questions!

Thankfully God loves it when we ask questions. He loves it when we care enough to find out why we are not walking in the blessing that He longs to pour out upon His people and upon the land. You may have some questions you need to be asking God, for your life or the corporate life of your community.

As we prayed and asked God lots of questions, He began to reveal to us that we usually live in the here and now. We do not always understand that we are part of history and that we stand on the shoulders of all those who have gone before us. What they did and how they lived their lives, affects our lives and what we do and how we live will impact future generations.

Using the environment as an example, it is easy for us to understand that how we live and the amount of pollution we produce, impacts our nations now and in the future.

How we live spiritually is similar - we can tend to pray in a very superficial way. We often pray for ourselves, our families or the usual prayer lists. We do not usually pray with an understanding of our family history or the history of our community and land. When you look at our history there is so much sin, so much abuse and pain. Where would you start to deal with the sin of a big city like Liverpool that has over 800 years of history? Should you even do anything about it? After all it's not your sin, is it?

One example of someone who stood in the gap before God for sin that was not his responsibility, is Jesus. He committed no sin. He did nothing wrong and yet the Bible tells us He died a cruel death taking upon Himself all of my sin and all of your sin.

Some people call this "Identificational Repentance". There are plenty of books written on this subject, but at that time I had not read any books or heard anyone speak about such things. Some people do not believe this sort of repentance is the right thing to do. However, all I can say is that we simply prayed and asked God for help. This is the journey He led us on and the amazing results speak for themselves.

So where do we begin? The Lord reminded me of the dandelions that grow rather too frequently in our gardens. We often deal with them by tugging at the flower or the stem while the root remains in the ground to flower many times again and to spread. Things can look neat and tidy on the surface of life but spiritually if the roots are not dealt with, there is an access point for Satan to bring destruction. In our lives it can mean we simply do not have the opportunity to walk in the fullness of God's blessing because we are contending with the consequences of other people's sin.

Sometimes we can be like the gardener who tries to dig up the dandelion in the winter. You could be digging all over the garden looking for the weeds with little joy. However, if you wait until the right time, when the dandelion raises its head above the ground, you will know exactly where it is and be able to root it out successfully.

For us our prayer journey has been like that...we have learnt to wait on the Lord to show us what is on His heart and how to deal with it. Then allow the Lord to show us what we need to do in order to release His goodness into our communities and cities.

God took us through His word and took us right back to biblical basics, to transform our thinking, our lives and our walk with Him forever. In the next chapter I want to share with you what we learnt.

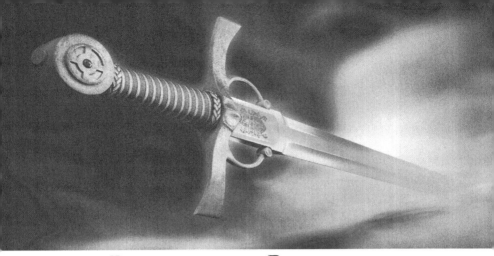

BACK TO BASICS

As we prayed, God took us back through the scriptures to the story of the fall of Satan, the creation of man and the epic saga of Adam and Eve. He took us through the story of Moses, the plagues and to the awesome story of Jesus coming to earth and then dying on the cross. When we started to understand and apply all that we had discovered, it changed our lives and I hope and pray it will do the same for you.

Satan was a beautiful angel and responsible for the worship in heaven. He became full of pride, considering himself more powerful than God and he became very wicked. There was no room in heaven for such evil so the Lord cast him down to earth.

Satan's power is not limitless! In fact he even had to ask God's permission before he could touch Job (read the story for yourself in Job 1:7-12). However we know from God's word that Satan can afflict and hinder God's people. In 1 Thessalonians 2:18 Paul tells the Thessalonians that he, Silas and Timothy wanted to go to them, but Satan blocked their way. But he is never ever allowed to block us completely or win an ultimate victory over us.

"In this world you will have trouble. But take heart! I have overcome the world." John 16:33

We know the end of the story and we are on the winning side!!!! Yeah!

If you are going through a difficult time, can I suggest that you press further into God? Ask Him what He wants to achieve in you or through you in the situation you find yourself in. As you press into God you will find that you will come through most situations quicker, than if you feel sorry for yourselves or focus your attention on Satan. Certainly that has been my experience. Satan is only ever allowed to touch our lives in order that God can direct us into an even greater measure of His love, provision or anointing.

Now let's take a look at what happened in the Garden of Eden:

God created man in His own image; in the image of God He created him; male and female He created them. Then God blessed them, and God said to them, "Be fruitful and MULTIPLY; fill the earth and subdue it; have DOMINION over the fish of the sea, over the birds of the air, and over every living thing that moves on the earth." Genesis 1:27-28 (NKJV)

We were created in the image of God. That is so good I need to say it again - you and I were created in the image of God! Yes it is true and we really need to believe it. Do we believe it? Do we live like that? Most of us know that is what the Scripture tells us, but we look in the mirror and despise what we see. We do not realise that as we reject ourselves, we are rejecting who God created us to be.

God created Adam and Eve, not just in His image, but also with DOMINION but what does that dominion mean? The dictionary's definition of dominion is "force, strength, might, manifested power, to perfect, to complete, inherent power, liberty of action, authority."

When God gave Adam and Eve dominion and authority, He gave them a powerful gift. Satan lost all his authority and power when he was thrown out of heaven and prowled the Garden of Eden, looking for his opportunity to steal that dominion and authority from Adam and Eve. Satan saw his opportunity and tempted Eve to eat the only fruit God had told them not to eat. As they did not resist the temptation, Adam and Eve disobeyed God, despite his lavish generosity to them. God was angry with them and cast Adam and Eve out of the garden. Satan's plan had worked and he took his opportunity to snatch the dominion and authority once held by Adam and Eve. Thankfully, we know that was not the end of the story.

THE BLOOD OF JESUS SETS THE CAPTIVES FREE

So we understand the importance of dominion and authority, and now we need to understand the power of Jesus. Let us return to the story of Moses who was a most unlikely hero, to help us to understand why we needed Jesus to come and why His blood had to be shed.

Moses said to God, "Who am I, that I should go to Pharaoh and bring the Israelites out of Egypt?" And God said, "I will be with you."
Exodus 3:11-12

Many of us feel just like Moses; who am I? Have you ever found yourself saying, "I cannot speak to these people! But God, I cannot do that!!!" God says He will never leave us or forsake us. Take courage as you see what God did through Moses.

As Moses and Aaron moved in obedience to God (always the key to success) there followed ten signs or plagues. They increased in severity, attacking the entire religious system of Egypt. They also displayed God's power to both the Egyptians and the children of Israel, who had been living with the Egyptian culture and gods for many years.

You can read about the final plague in Exodus 12 where God gave clear instructions. Each household had to prepare a healthy one year old male sheep or goat. At dusk on the fourteenth day of the month the entire community of Israel slaughtered their lambs. Some of the blood was then smeared on the two doorposts and the lintels of the houses where they were eating.

The blood was a sign that stopped death from entering the household; the spirit of death passed over and no disaster touched them. The meat of the lamb was eaten with bread, made without yeast and bitter herbs. They had to eat it quickly, ready to leave, fully dressed, with their sandals on and their sticks in their hands.

That night death visited Egypt, visiting every home and family including Pharaoh's, destroying every first born. However the power of the blood of the lamb that was slain saved the children of Israel. Tragically those not covered by the blood saw their firstborn die that night. God used this crisis to open the door of freedom for the children of Israel. Here began their journey to the Promised Land.

Through the blood of a sacrificial lamb, the Israelites received not only deliverance, but also healing and provision for the days ahead. Psalm 105:37 tells us that Israel came out, laden with silver and gold, and from among their tribes no one faltered. Millions of people, both young and old, walked out of Egypt whole; no cripples, no disease - that is our awesome God!

TRANSFER OF AUTHORITY

Thankfully that was not the end of the story, as God knew we would never make it on our own. He knew that we could never succeed by following the Ten Commandments and He loved us enough to send Jesus, the King of Heaven, our redeemer and Saviour, to earth on our behalf.

We know that Jesus came as the Lamb of God from heaven and He was very confident as He ministered here on earth. As He ministered He released heaven everywhere He went.

Heaven is a place of perfect love, love that is patient and kind. A place where there is no envy or boasting, no arrogance or rudeness. Heaven is a place of incredible intimacy and complete acceptance without hidden agendas. It is a place of holiness and awe where we see God for who He really is.

Heaven is a place outside of time and yet in control of time! Heaven is a place of wholeness, complete health and well being where there is NO sickness. Heaven is a place of truth, where there is no deception operating, where what is spoken will come to pass. A place of excellent strategies as God releases destinies over lives, families, communities and nations!

Heaven is a place of full provision where there is no lack or need. A place where there is no rejection or isolation. A place where there is no abuse, violence or death.

Heaven is such an amazing place, would you want to leave that place of perfection? Jesus' first sacrifice was to leave all of that behind, and to come to be born as a vulnerable human baby, open to all of the same problems that we are. He came to a broken world to release heaven to earth. He came to release people into the fullness of their heavenly destiny and gifts.

Jesus came to earth filled with the perfection of heaven - full of perfect love, full of healing, full of strategies for every different situation. He was never anxious or worried about what to do. Jesus knew how to release heaven to earth:

When John, who was in prison, heard about the deeds of the Messiah, he sent his disciples to ask him, 'Are you the one who is to come, or should we expect someone else?' Jesus replied, 'Go back and report to John what you hear and see: the blind receive sight, the lame walk, those who have leprosy are cleansed, the deaf hear, the dead are raised, and the good news is proclaimed to the poor.' Matthew 11:2-5

Jesus was thirty years old when he was baptised by John and filled with the Holy Spirit.

Jesus, full of the Holy Spirit, left the Jordan and was led by the Spirit into the wilderness, where for forty days he was tempted by the devil. He ate nothing during those days, and at the end of them he was hungry. The devil said to him, 'If you are the Son of God, tell this stone to become bread.' Jesus answered, 'it is written: "Man shall not live on bread alone." The devil led him up to a high place and showed him in an instant all the kingdoms of the world. And he said to him, 'I will give you all their authority and splendour; it has been given to me, and I can give it to anyone I want to. If you worship me, it will all be yours.' Luke 4:1-7

Jesus did not challenge Satan's authority because He knew the end of the story!

JESUS WON THE VICTORY

Every day Jesus released heaven to earth as he healed people and as he set people free of demonic bondage. Three years later the death of Christ on the cross was the grand climax to a sinless life. As Jesus hung upon the cross Satan thought he had won, but he suffered his greatest defeat as Jesus triumphed over sickness, death and sin, taking back the authority lost by Adam and Eve.

Jesus was our sacrificial lamb and He paid the price we could not. Jesus gave His blood in seven ways and the number seven represents completion.

The perfect sacrifice to satisfy God's holy wrath:

- Jesus sweat drops of blood – Luke 22:44
- Jesus' face bled as He was beaten – Luke 22:64
- Jesus bled as his beard was torn out – Isaiah 50:6
- Jesus bled from brutal scourging – Matthew 27:26
- Jesus' head bled from the crown of thorns – Matthew 27:29a

Charles Spurgeon said "There are no crown-wearers in heaven who were not cross-bearers here below".

- Jesus' hands and feet bled from the nails driven into them – Luke 23:33a
- Jesus bled from his side from the piercing of a Roman spear– John 19:34

Jesus paid a high price for you and for me. He is our deliverer and our healer. He is our rock and fortress! Jesus' leaving the perfection of heaven to die a painful death, was the ultimate sacrifice. It did not end there, as death could not hold him down and Jesus rose from the dead. Yeah! Hallelujah! Jesus' resurrection was so powerful, accomplishing far more than we will ever comprehend. That same power is available for you and for me. Have you taken hold of yours?

Our victory over Satan is to be seen in the cross of Christ, for it was there that God 'disarmed the principalities and powers," and it is through Jesus' blood shed on our behalf that we are able to overcome.

Jesus went to the cross and paid the price in full so we can engage with God and be a vessel to bring heaven to earth. Jesus rose again having completely destroyed the power of death.

Jesus Christ who has gone into heaven and is at the right hand of God, angels and authorities and powers have been made subject to Him. 1 Peter 3:22

Christ is far above all rule and authority and power and dominion, and above every name that is named. Certainly all things are under His feet.

If we need further evidence of Jesus' authority we need to read the Great Commission:

> *Jesus came and spoke to them, saying, "All authority has been given to Me in heaven and on earth. Go therefore and make disciples of all the nations, baptising them in the name of the Father and of the Son and of the Holy Spirit, teaching them to observe all things that I have commanded you; and lo, I am with you always, even to the end of the age."* Matthew 28:18-20

Now He lives in us through His Holy Spirit and chooses to move on the earth through you and through me. Wow! It is now our turn, not just to make history, but to create a better tomorrow.

We now know who Jesus is and comprehend the authority available for us to have dominion through Him. It is important to know that we are not just God's children or a part of the Bride of Christ but imperative that we understand how unique we are and that we have an amazing destiny.

• We are all original designer labels - Forget the Jimmy Choo shoes costing £895 a pair and the Precious Rose luxury handbags for £90,000, you are an original priceless gift from God to our nations! You are here to make a significant difference.

• You were on God's heart from the beginning of eternity. He knew the exact time and place you would be born. God had a purpose for bringing you into this world and for bringing you to the place where you live. We are not here for ourselves but created by God to release His presence, to release His creativity and to move in His authority.

• We need to understand what makes us unique. What makes you different from those around you?

• What are the gifts that we carry? How do we use them and improve them? How do we partner with each other and with those who have complimentary gifts to make a strong team? We need to honour each other and to make room for everyone to function in their gift.

We need to know how to position ourselves to bring heaven to earth. We need to understand how to take hold of the authority that Jesus took back from Satan. We need to learn how to use our authority! We need to know how to walk as God's children and as Ambassadors, in amazing humility and yet in our authority to release heaven to earth.

In his book "Don't Make History Change the Future" Matt Summerfield, Chief Executive of Urban Saints said:

> Every single one of us will make history but the big question is what kind of history are we going to make? Or maybe that's the wrong question because our history is someone else's future! So maybe the real question is not what history will I make, but what kind of future will I create? What legacy will I leave? What possibilities and opportunities will I have opened up for those who follow me?[2]

What will happen if we don't arise to the challenge? God wants to use us to bring glory to Him and to bring breakthrough once again for the people of our communities. He desires to bring healing and deliverance, to bring miraculous financial provision, to bring new business ideas, to be entrepreneurs, to be pioneers, to be creative, to bring to earth all the vision and creativity that is stored up in heaven. God wants to use us to pioneer new medical breakthroughs like the one being worked on right now to provide vaccine against malaria. God wants to use us - that is you and me - to bring heaven to earth.

So how do we do that? We do that by being naturally supernatural - by walking full of the Holy Spirit, aware of heaven's perfection, and expectant that we can be used by God to pull heaven to earth.

Danny Lee Silk in his book Culture of Honour writes:
> Sustaining a supernatural lifestyle, where signs and wonders follow us, is totally dependent on living out our true identities as sons and daughters of God.[3]

Jesus says to Peter "God himself, let you in on this secret of who I really am. And now I'm going to tell you who you are, really are. You are Peter, a rock. This is the rock on which I will put together my church, a church so expansive with energy that not even the gates of hell will be able to keep it out. And that's not all. You will have complete and free access to God's kingdom, keys to open any and every door: no more barriers between heaven and earth, earth and heaven. A yes on earth is yes in heaven and a NO on earth is a NO in heaven!" Matthew 16:17-19 (The Message)

IT'S TIME TO TAKE HOLD OF THE AUTHORITY

The great news in that something radical happened at the cross. Consequently, because of the death and resurrection of Jesus, we can now enjoy the position and authority in Him to resist Satan and to walk in freedom. That authority and freedom is not so we can do whatever we like and serve our own needs. It is so that we can serve the Lord and serve those He wants to touch through our lives. Jesus came not to be served but to serve and so should we.

Sadly, most of the time we do not live our lives as though God has given us dominion. Many of us live our lives like victims - victims of our past and fearful of the future. However, we need to believe what God says and discard the rubbish that other people have said. It is often a journey for us and it takes time to learn to think differently about ourselves and about others.

We also need to know that our personal victory depends on our will to resist Satan's temptations. We need to make healthy choices!

Stop lying to each other; tell the truth, for we are parts of each other and when we lie to each other we are hurting ourselves. If you are angry, don't sin by nursing your grudge. Don't let the sun go down with you still angry - get over it quickly; for when you are angry, you give a mighty foothold to the devil. Ephesians 4:25–27 (The Living Bible)

To help Christians win this battle against Satan, God has provided the power of Christ's blood.

And they overcame him by the blood of the Lamb and by the word of their testimony, and they did not love their lives to the death. Revelation 12:11 (NKJV)

We need to remind ourselves of this and remind Satan. The blood that Jesus shed on our behalf was overcoming blood! It carries the ability to overcome anything that Satan could ever use against God's people.

The Lord is so good to us and has revealed step by step the foundations of our faith from Adam and Eve - the loss of their dominion and authority, to how Jesus redeemed our lives and bought back that dominion and authority through the cross and the shedding of His blood. The trouble for most of us as Christians is that we don't comprehend what that really means for us. We don't know how to take hold of that dominion and authority, and how to use it to serve God humbly and effectively.

The earnest (heartfelt, continued) prayer of a righteous man makes tremendous power available (dynamic in its working). James 5:16 (Amplified)

I was desperate to see the power of God being manifested as the norm in our lives. The more I pressed into God, the more I could not bear to compromise what I believed the word of God said. That is not to say that I have got that right all of the time.

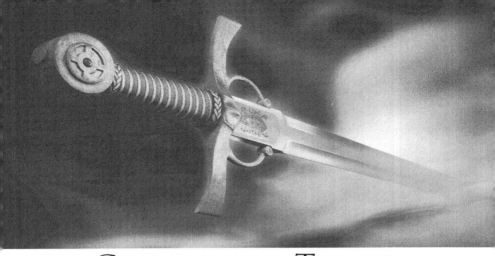

CHANGING TIMES

When we were not suffering major debt I was content with all that was provided for my family. We lived a simple life and it was not until I was attending an important family occasion, wearing a second hand dress, that someone challenged me by saying that God would want to provide for me to have a new dress. My response was that my dress was lovely and I was thrilled with it. However, this friend was challenging my mindsets that had no expectations of God wanting to bless us with new things. I had experienced so many disappointments that my levels of expectation had become very low and that way I was never going to be disappointed again. This dear friend loved us enough to provoke me to pray about it and ask God to deal with anything that was not His best for us.

My friend was right, God does want to bless us more than we are ready to receive. I actually believed that God wanted to bless other people. I had no problem at all with that and would happily pray such blessing for other people. The problem for me was that I could not believe that God wanted to really bless ME!

It was rooted in a life times' experience of rejection from my Dad and several others. God is our heavenly Father and He loves to give His children good things. Are there things Father God wants to bless you with that you have no confidence to ask Him for? Take a few minutes to think and pray about that.

For me, this was essential for the days ahead. I am sure that if I had not been willing to allow God to deal with my low levels of expectation then He would not have been able to use me so powerfully in the future.

A time of great breakthrough for us came as I read "Blessings and Curses – You Can Choose" written by Derek Prince.[4] It provides simple teaching about what is a curse and how you can identify if there is one operating in your family's life. We need to deal with any curses and release the blessings. If you have one or two of these things in your life it does not necessarily mean there is a curse there. However if you have several on the list, you need to ask the Lord if there is something there that needs to be dealt with.

The signs of a curse Derek Prince mentioned were:
- Mental and or emotional breakdown.
- Repeated or chronic sickness (especially if hereditary).
- Barrenness, a tendency to miscarry, or related female problems.
- Breakdown of marriage and family alienation.
- Continuing financial insufficiency.
- Being "accident-prone".
- A history of suicides and unnatural or untimely deaths.

I knew that we had at least six of those operating strongly in both my Mum's and Dad's families and in my life too. In his book, Derek Prince illustrates how a curse can operate throughout different generations of a family.

For the curse to be broken, it takes someone to pray and repent for any wrong things done by members of the family historically. Some examples of those wrong things could be involvement in freemasonry, witchcraft or the occult, sexual sin or idolatry to name but a few. As I read the book I asked the Holy Spirit if there were any family issues that I needed to repent of and I prayed through the simple prayers from the book. I believe God used this book very powerfully to change my life dramatically and it was the beginning of the end of poverty controlling our lives. Thank you Father God for your provision for us.

If you recognise any of those issues operating in your life I recommend this book to you and there are other materials around to help. I suggest that you take some time to deal with any issues that may hold you back from all the great things that God has for you and your family.

TIME WITH SELWYN

I was invited to go down to a leaders' training week with Selwyn Hughes in Waverley Abbey. I arrived to discover that the rest of the leaders were Vicars, Curates and Ministers which immediately left me feeling intimidated and totally out of my depth. However, Selwyn was wonderful, encouraging everyone including me, to fulfil our potential. To my surprise, God used me very powerfully in ministering to almost every person there with a prophetic word of encouragement or a word of knowledge that brought real breakthrough for each individual.

I was surprised and thrilled that God was using me there, but I still did not know what God was going to do for me. On the final afternoon we had communion together and as we left Waverley Abbey, Selwyn took hold of my hand just as a Father takes a child's hand. He said his farewells to others as they left but he did not let go of my hand. Something very strange was happening to me that I did not understand at the time, but now I know that God was preparing me for a major breakthrough.

We said goodbye and I stayed in my brother's house that night, as he lived on my route home. The Lord woke me up at 3am and I asked Him what had been happening when Selwyn was holding my hand the previous day. I began to repent thinking that maybe I was impressed with a man of Selwyn's stature holding my hand. I could feel the warmth of God's love pouring over me, and His smile radiating towards me. The Lord said to me that I had not gone to Waverley Abbey thinking I may be rejected by men, I had gone expecting everyone to reject me. Wow that was so true and I had not realised it!

I began to sob as the extravagant fire of God touched my life. As the fire came, the weight of the years of rejection from my Dad and many others began to be exposed and slide off my shoulders. The Lord loved on me for a couple of hours, as I watched scenes from my life being played out before me, like scenes in a theatrical play. Each time the curtains opened, another scene from my life was revealed. I clearly remember watching as the Lord showed me my nineteenth birthday: I was sitting sobbing on my bed in Steve's home. My parents were continuing to ignore me and had not even sent me a birthday card. Suddenly the pain and rejection that had been bottled up for years came flooding to the surface. I was shocked at how I had buried the pain so deeply. I did not feel angry or bitter but instantly I knew I had to release forgiveness to them and bless them (even though my Dad had already died by this point).

Again and again the stage curtains of my life drew back with different scenes of where I had been rejected. This included the church who had refused to help when I was a young child trying to deal with the pain of the domestic violence; my Dad's extended family who had turned their backs on us; teachers and bullies at school; those who had sexually abused me; and many more.

I was amazed at how much pain I had been trying to live with buried so deep down inside. I took time to release forgiveness and blessing to each person. I did that even though they had never shown any remorse or made any effort to apologise. Forgiveness is not dependent upon our feelings but an act of our will and so it comes down to a simple choice - do we choose to forgive or not. Many people end up emotionally, physically and spiritually crippled because they have not released forgiveness from past hurts. If you have any unforgiveness in your heart, please have the courage to face the situation. Do what you can to resolve it and to release forgiveness as soon as is practically possible.

I immediately felt completely different as so much of the rejection washed off me and I received acceptance and love from Father God. As I returned home I felt like a new person and I was! Immediately several people saw the difference, asking what had happened to me as they said I looked ten years younger!

Rejection is very hard to bear but you need to know that no matter how much man rejects you, God never will. He loves you! He loves you! He loves you!

See what great love the Father has lavished on us, that we should be called children of God! 1 John 3:1

And that is what we are. The Bible says it, so it must be true - awesome!

You really can choose to walk in forgiveness and blessing and receive your adoption into God's family. Father God promises never to leave you or forsake you, that is His word and He never lies. When we do not receive God's healing we become people who draw rejection and the pattern of life continues with hurt and conflict. I encourage you to deal with rejection if that has been part of your story too. If we depend on our feelings we will never do it and will end up lonely and full of bitterness.

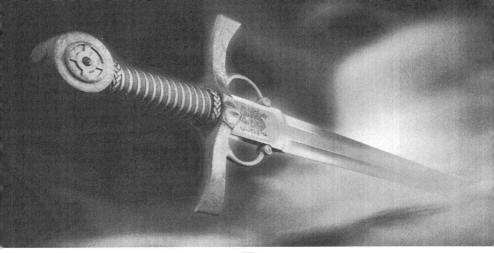

POWER OF DECEPTION

Telling my story is difficult because it is not just my story but a story that affects other people too. I was urged to write this because the Lord wants to use my experience of brokenness to show others they can choose not to be a victim. You can choose to be a survivor and overcome the most painful and difficult of times. You can allow what God says about your future to shape your present life and not the traumas of your past. How we react in these painful times will shape our future. One of the areas I found very difficult for many years was the situation that I am about to relate.

I also tell this story, as I am desperate to see the bride prepared for Jesus. Throughout the Bible, God talks about His people and His church, describing them as the bride and Jesus as the Bridegroom.

> *Let us rejoice and be glad and give Him glory! For the wedding of the Lamb has come, and his bride has made herself ready.* Revelation 19:7

To make ourselves ready for the Bridegroom, we have to stop turning a blind eye to the wrong things that happen. The more we turn a blind eye and sweep things under the carpet, the dirtier the bridal garment becomes.

If we really want to be a part of that beautiful Bride we need to be walking in real humility. We need to be prepared when necessary to break the silence. We need to welcome truth so that we can repent of our sin and come together in real unity that is deep and strong. I am open to discussion on all that we have experienced, but after many years and numerous attempts on our part, the others involved in the story have sadly not been willing to meet.

Shortly after arriving in Waterloo we were enjoying being a part of a wonderful House Group with brilliant and inspiring leaders. I thank God for them as I learnt so much from them. It was a mixed group of people and we spent many happy hours together.

However, for me it all began to change when one evening, as a young woman called Ann began to share about her Mum. Suddenly the penny began to drop, this was the daughter of Mary, the lady my Dad had the affair with a few years earlier. She spoke of her little brother and I realised that this was actually my half-brother. It quickly became clear to me that Ann knew nothing of the affair. I was hit with panic and despair and God alone managed to keep me together for the rest of the meeting. I had no idea what to do and where to go. I had no idea how Ann would respond if she knew the truth. I was confused; how should we handle these things as Christians who believe in living in the truth?

I eventually plucked up the courage to go to see our House Group Leaders and poured out the whole heartbreaking story through floods of tears. They were shocked and advised me to go to see our Pastor, to seek his wisdom. The Pastor advised that as Mary did not come to the church, it should not be a problem, as her daughter was about to move away. So Ann moved away without knowing anything about the past and I hoped that would be the end of the crisis.

However, that was not to be, as a little while later Mary gave her life to Jesus and started coming to church with her young son Tom. Mary was frequently brought out to the front of the Church to share her powerful testimony, of how Jesus had saved her from a desperate life of alcohol abuse and brokenness, and He had. It was a wonderful testimony, however the whole time I was filled with utter panic as so many people from Alcoholics Anonymous and some members of my family knew the truth about her little son. What would happen when other people found that out? Mary had a lot of family and friends within the church, so I found it very difficult.

I decided to talk to Mary about what had happened, as I believed that as Christians we should walk in the truth. She admitted the truth to me and begged me to keep it secret, as she did not want her husband to find out. I had great compassion for her and after all she was born again and had started her life afresh. Yet I could not settle with this and I felt I was being dragged into the deception. Deception is not like an intentional lie, it is far more subtle than that. It is a disguising of the truth so it cannot be seen. Until truth comes and brings everything into the light, things that are wrong appear right when deception is operating.

A Biblical example of this would be the story of Ananias and Sapphira found in Acts 5. Christians at that time were selling all they had so they could live together in community and use their resources for the kingdom. Ananias and Sapphira sold their home and kept some of the money back for themselves. When Ananias presented the money to the apostles Peter said "Ananias, how is it that Satan has so filled your heart that you have lied to the Holy Spirit and have kept for yourself some of the money you received for the land?" As a result of their action they were killed stone dead; not by man, but by God! Now that really scared me!!!

I met with the Pastor who said that one day the truth would come out but not yet. Meanwhile Tom became a great friend of my children, coming to stay the night as young friends do.

I felt that Mary had placed the burden of responsibility of the consequences of her husband finding out upon my shoulders. He had a heart condition and

I felt great sorrow, grief and compassion for him. I was told that if anything happened to him as a result of him finding out Tom was not his child, it would be on my head! It was very easy for people to do that to me, as I was still taking on the responsibility of the world. After all, that was what I had been forced to do from a young age.

However, I hated being forced to live in deception and felt ashamed that I was allowing my children to be deceived too. My children simply thought Tom was their friend and not their Uncle. I truly believed that if we had given this painful situation to God, then He would have been able to bring cleansing, healing and reconciliation for all. After all, our God is the God of the impossible.

I struggled desperately with this very sad state of affairs. I did not want to see this family hurt. I had forgiven Mary and my Dad for the affair. After all they had just been two very messed up people who had sought comfort in the wrong places and they had both repented. So for me that was not an issue. The issue for me was the on-going deception and the longer it went on the worse it felt. The Bible tells us "you should know the truth and truth will set you free". How could there be freedom for anyone in this sad situation when we were all walking in deception? I felt like I was walking with a huge thundercloud above my head that I had no control over and that could release lightening bolts to destroy all of our lives at any time.

My Mum was very angry and desperate to come to church and blow the whole thing out of the water. My brother who was not a Christian could not understand that Christians would cover this up. It really made him angry with me that I defended the Pastor and Mary, who appeared to simply brush everything under the carpet. Spiritually I thought I was doing the right thing in honouring my Pastor and coming under his authority year after year, but in the end it cost my family and I dearly.

Over time, friendships blossomed naturally between Tom and my children, given that they were in the same age group and spent lots of time together at church. I hated feeling that I was being dishonest with my own children, as they were oblivious to the facts. I felt I was deceiving them and I was.

As the years went by, I tried to bury the truth and stay submitted to the authority of our Pastor. However, our church started a wonderful course called "Freedom In Christ"[5] which led to a "Freedom Appointment". This encouraged everyone to deal with any issues that could be causing a blockage in their spiritual lives. It covers things like ancestral curses, idolatry, false religions, witchcraft, hurt and unforgiveness.

During my Freedom Appointment I was encouraged to share my story and the whole situation just poured out, as it was always heavy on my heart, pulling me down. The situation with Mary and Tom was out of my control and therefore there was no help to relieve me of the burden I was carrying. Once again I struggled with maintaining the deception - I simply could not understand how it was biblical to do this. I felt hopeless and trapped by deception that was not mine. There were no solutions offered, so it simply got buried again and I had to try to maintain the pretence.

As the years went by I still could not understand that our holy, awesome God would want this deception to continue. Our children were now teenagers and I made it clear that if Tom approached my daughter for a date, then I would have to tell my children the truth. I was laughed at for saying that, until some time later Tom said he had feelings for my daughter and he was going to ask her to be his girlfriend. Tom told his Mum and Mary was forced to tell him the truth, but he was asked to keep it a secret from his Dad. The deception was growing and affecting more people.

How painful and difficult for these precious youngsters! Neither of them deserved the pain they have experienced because of other people's problems.

It was only by accident that I found out that Tom had been told the truth. I was dismayed, as I did not want my children to find out from the gossips.

So with heavy hearts, Steve and I poured out the story to our children and I apologised to them for not telling them the truth earlier. We all wept together and now they too were involved with the deception, as Mary's husband still did not know the truth!

It is desperately sad that the mistakes of others have such a traumatic impact on the lives of those who were completely innocent. I felt desperately sorry for them all.

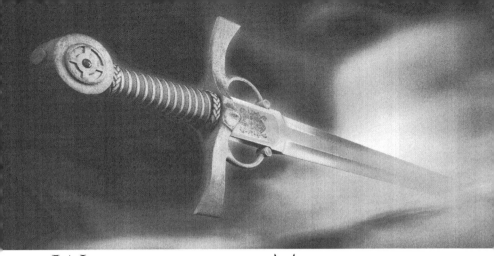

WORKPLACE MIRACLES

I have always made myself available to serve God 24/7, no matter where I have been. Sometimes we are the only opportunity people have to encounter the presence of God. I worked within Local Government in a small office part-time and shortly before I left the job, I heard the Lord clearly instruct me to offer to pray for one of the girls who sat opposite me.

Angela was a formidable girl who was desperate for a baby. I was very apprehensive about what her response would be. When I asked her if she would like me to pray for her, Angela almost ran out of the room. Not the most encouraging response I have ever had!

She stood in the doorway and said she would welcome my prayers but for me to pray for her when I was at home. I felt very humiliated and embarrassed but it was never about me. It was always about how much Jesus loved Angela.

I moved from that job within the month and forgot all about her. However God had not! Four months later Angela rang and we made arrangements to meet for lunch as she said she had some great news for me. Her Father had died in front of her when she was only thirteen years old and she had not had a period since then. The doctors had told her it was impossible for her to conceive. However, exactly one month from the day I offered to pray for her, Angela had her first period in many years. She thought it was just a blip as she did not have another one, but it only took one period for her to fall pregnant. Angela had a healthy pregnancy before giving birth to a beautiful little boy. That's my God! He is the God of the miraculous who particularly likes to touch the unsaved with His love and power.

A couple of years later the Lord laid her on my heart once again to pray for another baby. I prayed and then waited to see what God would do. A few months later I bumped into Angela and she said she had something to tell me. Yes you guessed it, she was pregnant again and this time she went on to have a little girl. Praise the Lord!

Another example of God's goodness occurred when one of our staff came into work as white as a sheet and obviously in a lot of pain. Bob was one of those cheeky chaps and rather flirtatious. You did not know whether, if you took him up on any of his offers, you would be in serious trouble, or he would run a mile! I could not bear to see him in so much pain and so took courage and offered to pray for him. He had terrible arthritic pain in his knee and it was very swollen. I took him into a room praying like mad "please let this be of you Lord or I am going to be in big trouble". I quickly explained that I was going to ask God to show Bob how much He loves him by healing his knee. I laid my hand on Bob's knee, simply prayed and immediately God dramatically touched Bob's knee. The swelling that had been all around the knee completely disappeared, and all the pain went. Bob was overwhelmed and to this day still says that God healed him.

In the year 2000, the Lord spoke to me about laying down my paid employment so that I could be available to serve Him full-time. By this point we had finished the ministry with the Puppet Theatre. So it seemed a strange time for God to say that, as our finances were not good and we needed my salary to support our income. Steve threw down an impossible gauntlet to the Lord. He did not appreciate just how good God is at the impossible! Steve stated, "If God gave him a job with an increase of salary that covered the loss of my salary, then I could leave my job." No problem to God!

So, I did not strive or try to persuade Steve, I simply put my trust in God because He is so good at the impossible. Only God could either change Steve's mind or provide the amount Steve stated.

A few weeks later, Steve came home from work with the grim news that he was about to be made redundant. They told him that there was a slim chance, that he could be offered a position in Heysham, a small port further up the coast from where we live. That would mean a one and a half hour journey to work and so would realistically have meant us relocating. We did not believe that the Lord wanted us to relocate and there did not appear to be any other options.

As we prayed, we kept getting the sense that God was up to something and soon after Steve was called into the office. To our surprise his boss offered Steve a job working on the Douglas oil and gas platform located eighteen miles offshore in Liverpool Bay. It would mean Steve going to work in a helicopter and he would be away from home for two weeks at a time. The good news was that he would be home for two weeks after that and the salary would be enough to cover my salary with a little bit more. God had certainly risen to the challenge and I was able to hand in my notice to leave my paid employment.

Soon after, I was given a scripture which was the scripture that Jesus actually quoted in Luke 4:18-19. This is one of my favourite passages of scripture:

"The Spirit of the Sovereign Lord is on me, because the Lord has anointed me to proclaim good news to the poor. He has sent me to bind up the brokenhearted, to proclaim freedom for the captives

and release from darkness for the prisoners, to proclaim the year of the Lord's favor and the day of vengeance of our God, to comfort all who mourn, and provide for those who grieve in Zion - to bestow on them a crown of beauty instead of ashes, the oil of joy instead of mourning, and a garment of praise instead of a spirit of despair. They will be called oaks of righteousness, a planting of the Lord for the display of his splendor." Isaiah 61:1-3

The next verse is so powerful!

"They will rebuild the ancient ruins and restore the places long devastated; they will renew the ruined cities that have been devastated for generations." Isaiah 61:4

I love these verses as they tell each one of us that the Spirit of the sovereign Lord is upon US and that WE have been anointed to preach good news to the poor. WE have been sent to bind up the broken hearted, to proclaim freedom for the captives and release from darkness for the prisoners, to proclaim the year of the Lord's favour.

This is talking prophetically about Jesus, but actually it is also talking about you and me too. I am anointed and so are you, because the Spirit of the Sovereign Lord is upon us and we have been anointed to preach the good news to the poor. Please Lord, help us to walk in your anointing and to be carriers of your good news.

Isaiah 61 spoke to me of Liverpool and how the church needed to arise. How we as the church need to rebuild the ancient ruins and restore the places long devastated. How we need to bring renewal to the ruined city that was devastated years ago. This passage still speaks to me, of the transforming power of God that is released when God's people take hold of His Word and apply it to their land and community.

I literally looked at the devastated areas of our city of Liverpool in the year 2000 and prayed this word "the ancient ruins WILL BE rebuilt and the city will be RESTORED."

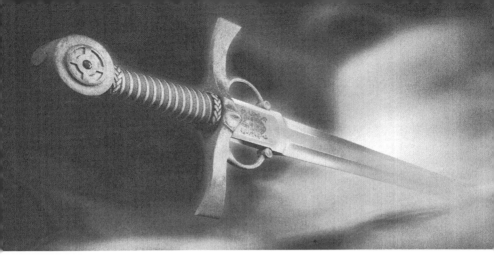

A LIGHTNING BOLT

As I left my job, I had no idea of what God had in store for me; all I had was a completely clean sheet waiting for Him to write on. Our church was just about to launch Neighbourhood Houses of Prayer and I was asked to take the lead in that. We encouraged people to form small groups to pray for three people each, who could be family members, neighbours, friends or colleagues. That felt good, but not enough to have a substantial transforming impact outside the walls of the church. So I decided we would also pray each month for a different organisation working within our community. Prior to the launch, we wrote to our local Police station. We advised them that we would be praying for them and asked them if there was anything in particular we could pray for.

A couple of weeks later I went in to see the Police, as they had not responded to my letter. (They had probably never had anyone wanting to pray for them before!) They sent a Probationary Officer out to meet me and I asked him if there was anything we could pray for them. He said, "Could you ask God for a bolt of lightening?" I thought it was a bit of a strange request, so I just smiled and said we would only be praying for their protection and success in detection, etc.

However, three days later, there was a huge storm over the area and the Police station was hit with a huge bolt of lightening! Thankfully, nobody was hurt but it really got their attention. Later I asked them, "Did it hit where you wanted it to and was it powerful enough?" This was the start of my relationship with the Police and unsurprisingly they took us more seriously after this!

As we continued to develop the work of the Neighbourhood Houses of Prayer, I began to research our community so that we could pray informed prayers. I looked at the age distribution, housing, employment, crime and health. All of this information is found easily on the internet and I was staggered at the results of my research. Local people were dying prematurely from cancers, suicide, stroke and coronary heart disease, plus the fertility rate was very poor. Why? There was no logical explanation for the poor health of our community, as there was no local source of contamination to cause such poor health. Could it be something to do with the death over the area that the Lord had shown us as we had walked the streets a few years earlier? I was soon to discover some answers to my questions and receive some keys to see this all change for good.

PROPHETIC REVELATION

During 2001, a prophet called Martin Scott came to the north Liverpool area with a "Sowing Seeds For Revival" team. Martin spoke about the history of the land, the causes of curses coming upon the land and how to cleanse the land. It was very similar to how a curse comes upon a person, and could be broken in the same way. Suddenly, everything began to make sense, as the reason for the poor health and high mortality rates could be due to a curse upon our land. I knew that God had not fallen asleep or overlooked us, but there were serious causes for the curse manifesting upon our people.

One of those causes was that Liverpool was one of the major ports in the slave trade and lots of the main political leaders of the time were heavily involved.

I had been crying out to God for understanding and revelation. During his first visit to Liverpool, Martin gave me a personal prophecy. He simply came and placed his hand upon my head and said "EXPANSION". Whoa! I felt like a balloon suddenly began to inflate inside me and I immediately received an incredible impartation which brought with it revelation and understanding.

Life was never the same after that. Several months later Martin returned and gave me two personal prophetic words, which together said that the Lord would use me to raise up a mobile Prayer School, which would cover the whole of the Mersey region.

During this second trip, Martin also gave a very strong prophetic word to Liverpool. He said that it was a key moment in the history of our region and he challenged us to get involved in its future. Martin said: "It is a pregnant moment in history when the church can begin to shape the city through prayer and action. Restrictions can be placed upon the demonic powers and piece-by-piece, step-by-step into the places of power will come those who will serve the AGENDA of JESUS. The economics will be affected and that which was not given to Liverpool before will then begin to be released. Also where there are financial injustices, economics will begin to be put right because wherever in scripture they hit the powers, in the heavens above, there is always economic repercussions".

He spoke of Liverpool becoming not just the Capital of Culture but also a European Capital. In June 2003 in the midst of great competition from other great cities, we were chosen to be the European Capital of Culture for 2008 using "the world in one city" as the strap line for our bid. Throughout the region there were great celebrations and the leader of the Liverpool Council spoke of a new day where a line had been drawn upon the past.

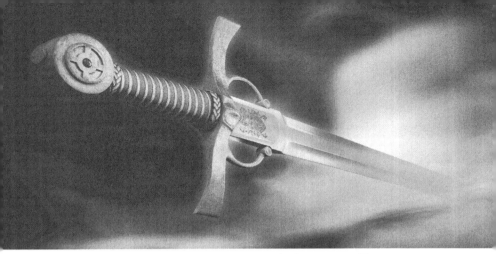

Taking Back The Land

During Spring 2002 our Neighbourhood Houses of Prayer Team started to prayer walk our community that included 162 roads and 5,642 homes. We repented that we had not used the authority that the Lord had given us to have dominion over our land. We had allowed the enemy to take territory, which belonged to the Lord. We took back the responsibility as the "Gatekeepers" of the land and declared what would be allowed to come in and out of our land.

Within a couple of months we had a big challenge. The North West Highways Agency and the local authority decided to close one of our roads. This was a very bad decision for the community and would cause chaos. They consulted the local community's opinion by posting a notice on a lamppost at the road junction and by putting tiny notices in the back pages of the local newspaper. But if you do not read the notices on the lampposts (for some that would mean getting out of your car to read it) or scrutinise the back pages of your local newspaper, you could miss some major consultation for your community!

As local people, we knew this was going to be very bad for our community. The roads were already very congested and if one of our exit roads was closed off, it would make it much worse. Ease of entry and exit from the area was required for those using the local hospital providing renal services and physiotherapy. We also had a constant flow of traffic accessing the library and the theatre, plus the private eye hospital, the mental health unit, several facilities for the elderly including residential and day care services. On top of that there was a Recycling Centre, offices and several hundred family homes.

With all of that in mind, we immediately challenged the decision. The local council and Highways Agency explained to me that they were the "experts" with all the computer programs to demonstrate how it would all work and they knew what they were doing. I was informed that it was too late to do anything about it and the work had already been approved and been put out to tender.

I had never been involved in anything of this nature before but knew this to be a dreadful decision, which would be very detrimental to our whole community. So I gathered a small team of residents together and we mobilised the local community to challenge the decision. We began a campaign to reverse the decision, complete with suggestions of how the road could actually be improved. We felt as though we were fighting Goliath, but we knew that with a small stone David brought freedom for the children of Israel and we needed freedom for our community.

We had six weeks before the work was due to start and so we had to act quickly. We gathered a petition with over twelve hundred names on it and mobilised the whole local community. We recruited the help of our local Councillor, who later, through this process, became a Christian.

We held a public meeting to advise the community of our action and progress. We emphasised clearly that it was essential that we received their full support if we were to succeed. The council called a special meeting, to which the Highways Agency and local community were invited to attend to discuss the whole issue. I was asked to speak on behalf of our community. I prepared a report that was to be presented in front of our community, the Council and the Highways Agency. Help!

I was really frightened, as I had never done anything like this before and our community were depending on me to present a good case. I prayed knowing that if it were dependant upon me we would fail. I called upon God to anoint me and to guide me through the process. What happened next took us all by surprise - especially me!

As I was speaking, I was so aware of all the eyes in the room being on me, as people listened intently. The press, Councillors, admin staff, the local Police Inspector, Mark Brew, and members of our local community were all busy taking notes. The atmosphere was very scary and you could have heard a pin drop, beside my voice presenting our case. Suddenly the Chair of the Councillors rose to his feet. He walked across to one of the other Councillors and they started a conversation.I was desperate that they should hear our whole presentation in order to make a wise decision but how could they do that when they were talking and not listening?

Oh my goodness! I did not know what to do as the conversation continued. I gently heard the Lord tell me to stop speaking and to explain that I did not wish to interrupt the Councillor's conversation. I took a big breath, I obeyed God and I said exactly what the Lord had told me to say. I thought I was going to die, as my heart was beating so loudly, I thought everyone could hear it. There was a sharp intake of breath as the whole room gasped and stared at the Councillors, who hurriedly shuffled back to their seats, apologised and invited me to continue.

The representative from the Highways Agency rose to his feet and responded to our presentation, once again stating that they were the experts and it had already gone out to tender. Then, finally the Councillors spoke together before announcing that they wished to overturn their previous decision to close the road. Not only was the decision overturned, but also they approved the suggestions that we had made for how the roads could be improved. The room erupted as the pressure was lifted and the whole community applauded the decision. I was thrilled and so grateful to the Lord for his help. What I did not know was the impression it had left with Inspector Mark Brew who the Lord had arranged for me to meet a few months later.

I was invited to apply to become a Councillor but I knew that was not something the Lord wanted me to do. However, an opportunity arose for me to get involved in the Sefton Local Strategic Partnership (LSP), so I applied and was successful. Sefton is next to Liverpool and the borough that I live in.

Serving on the LSP gave me the opportunity to work with the strategic Directors for the Health Authority, the Police and Fire Service, local Transport, Business, Education, Housing, Environmental Health and Social Services etc., and to be a part of planning the future. I was thrilled to be able to participate and to impact some of the most influential people in our region. My willingness to serve in this sphere released great favour on me.

PRAYING FOR OUR COMMUNITY

The local church community was made up of two areas, Waterloo and Seaforth, that together make up our political boundary, called Church Ward. I sensed that there was a very major stronghold and blockage over the area and suspected it was coming from Seaforth. I did not know what it was or why it was there but could nevertheless sense it.

With a little bit of research, I discovered that in 1813, John Gladstone had a home built for his family where he could see the beautiful beaches and sunsets. For those who do not know Liverpool, we do have beaches and fabulous sunsets! I looked at the historical maps of the region to discover its exact location. I found out that Seaforth was actually named after John Gladstone's Father-in-Law, Lord Seaforth, who was the Head of the MacKenzie Clan in Scotland. His family had been responsible for the attempted murder and rebellion against Queen Elizabeth I, in an attempt to put Mary upon the throne.

John Gladstone himself was an MP, a major slave trader and father of William Gladstone, four times the Prime Minister of Great Britain. Interestingly, the site of the house and the gardens became the very heart of Seaforth. Many years later, Seaforth was torn in half to make way for a dual carriageway called the Princess Way, but it is also known as the European Gateway that leads down to the entrance of one of the largest Freeports in Europe.

This was the area most affected by poor health, premature deaths and severe mental health problems. I believed that there was a significant connection between the history of the land and the current situation. We began to pray and to seek the Lord about the way forward in dealing with this. We continued to prayer walk the rest of the area and spent time preparing ourselves for carrying out the Seaforth walk.

I arranged to meet with Martin Scott to chat about our plans. Martin encouraged me to go for it, knowing that as we humbled ourselves before God, He would hear the cries of our hearts for the land and the people who lived there. Martin also said that as we were going to deal with the sin upon the land, God would also give us the anointing that was in the land. As Seaforth House had been the home of the Gladstones, there would be a strong anointing and authority for government. Martin believed that God was going to give that to me, as I was serving governmentally upon our Local Strategic Partnership and with the Police.

I have to confess that when Martin said that, it completely went over the top of my head and I did not understand what he was saying. I just smiled, nodded and said, "Oh that's nice"! However, despite me not understanding what was about to happen, God was certainly speaking through Martin and He did give me that anointing and authority for government, as you will read further on and hear about in the next book.

After much preparation, in September 2002 we prayer walked the Seaforth area. People from three of the local churches walked and prayed together. Before we started we took communion together as an act of real unity and love for one another. We repented for the death, murder, rape and enslavement that had been part of the origins of the name of Seaforth. We repented on behalf of the church leaders that had accepted slave money for the construction of local churches. We believe that something really shifted in the heavenlies over the region that evening.

In Acts 1:8 Jesus said to the disciples:

> *"But you will receive power when the Holy Spirit comes on you; and you will be my witnesses in Jerusalem, and in all Judea and Samaria, and to the ends of the earth."*

This verse was to become our pattern as it means that filled with the power of God, you start ministering in your local community to see things change for good, before you expand into your region, then your nation and then the ends of the earth. We started our ministry locally in the area surrounding our Church, which seemed vast to us at the time. The lessons the Lord taught us locally, He then stretched us to apply across the region, as the Lord then expanded our territory to Liverpool. Later we started to minister across the nation before we were invited to the nations.

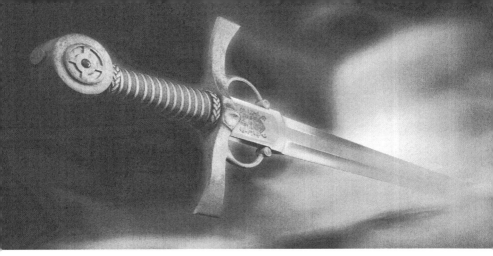

OUTRAGEOUS ANSWERS

"For our struggle is not against flesh and blood, but against the rulers, against the authorities, against the powers of this dark world and against the spiritual forces of evil in the heavenly realms." Ephesians 6:12

There is a spiritual battle going on around us, so we need to use our spiritual authority and weapons. We do not need to live in hopelessness and we do not need to allow what goes on in our communities to spiral out of control. As the Body of Christ, God created us to have dominion and we do that through prayer and action.

One of my favourite quotes is from Edmund Burke who said, "All it takes for evil to triumph is for good men to do nothing!" If we come before God with clean hands and pure hearts, we have the ability in God to exercise dominion and to do something good. As God's children we should be using the power of prayer that is available to us through Jesus, to shift our communities back to God.

Nobody has an ambition in life to become a drug addict. They have fallen for the oldest deception in the book "take this it's good for you". Satan's tactics never change. However, Jesus died for everyone who has ever lived and will ever live. Jesus paid the price for the sins of those whose lives are broken or messed up, just like He did for ours.

Many people have seen the amazing scenes in the first Transformations video[6] where God moved mightily and miraculously in Cali, Columbia in the battle against drugs. Produced by George Otis Jnr. these videos have inspired faith that God can move in our communities. We know that God has no favourites and that He loves the people of Merseyside, or any other community, just as much. All that is needed is for the church to call on God and obey what He says.

Early in 2002 a letter from the Chief Constable of Merseyside Police, Norman Bettison, was leaked to the press that said, "Merseyside is now the Drugs Distribution Capital of the UK". I was devastated as things across Merseyside at that time were already grim. I wondered why anyone would want to invest in our region if that was our reputation? As I cried out to God He said, "It's time for the church to ARISE and to declare a STOP and a turning of this tide of evil". Being a practical person I said to the Lord, "OK how are we going to do that?"

The Lord encouraged me to contact our local Councillor, who had become a Christian through the dispute over the road. Carol just so happened to also be the Chair of the Merseyside Police Authority. I gave her a call and she was only too willing to arrange a meeting for me with the Local Police Inspector, Mark Brew. Mark was lovely and pleased to meet up with me and he spoke of my incredible courage at the earlier Council meeting about the road. Incredible courage, he obviously hadn't seen how scared I was!

We sat and chatted over a cup of tea about what the Lord had put on my heart. Mark was very willing to be the Police representative and to meet up with me regularly. As we met, together we began to identify issues that we could mobilise the church to pray about. The Lord unveiled a very simple strategy and within three days DrugsNET was born.

DrugsNET was a very simple network of churches, prayer groups and individuals mobilised to pray. We would mobilise prayer about specific targets established as we met regularly with officers from Merseyside Police. We mobilised hundreds of people although we never met together en masse. We prayed within our own churches, groups and homes. We produced a prayer letter each month, including answers to prayer to encourage everybody and with the current prayer targets.

In case you want to use this idea for your community, here are some of the prayer targets we used:

- The young people of the region and the protection of their schools.
- The drug distribution networks e.g. the roads, rail networks, docks and airports.
- The drug gang leaders - we know of several gang leaders who became Christians and are now being used powerfully by God.
- The protection of our Police and their families and for them to have wisdom and insight.
- The addicts and those who prostitute themselves to finance their supplies.
- Those ministering to drug addicts.

There were many incredible and miraculous answers to prayer and a major work of bridge building with Merseyside Police. We saw huge seizures, arrests and an increase of resources for Merseyside Police to assist them with the 300% increase in information that came to them during 2003. It was great to see the crime rate drop dramatically as the Police had greater success. We believe that this was one of the keys to the transformation of our region.

Here are just a couple of stories to encourage you that our mighty God is simply looking for those who will stand in the gap and pray so that He can bring change.

The first story occurred in the Croxteth and Norris Green area of Liverpool in March 2003. This community is in Liverpool's North Policing area and at that time had the worst crime figures in Merseyside. The history of this community was a very sad one, as it was an area of great deprivation and had the worst housing. In fact the housing was so bad that it had been scheduled some years ago to be demolished and beautiful new homes built in its place. However, for whatever reasons the regeneration work was never done. Time and time again the residents had their hopes built up only to be disappointed, until they stopped hoping. Major hopelessness, despair and rejection set in resulting in a community with a lot of anger and bitterness. Given that the plan eventually was to demolish them, their homes were left as the Council did not want to invest in improvements. As the housing conditions deteriorated, the hopelessness and anger got much worse.

Gangs who pedalled drugs, guns and knives troubled the Norris Green and Croxteth communities. They left many of the innocent residents completely terrified. The gang leaders recruited young boys to cycle around the estates delivering their drugs for them and these youngsters earned a substantial income from that. Their school attendance was poor as there was no aspiration to get a good education; after all they had an income from dealing drugs. The Croxteth Crew and the Strand Gang, as they were known, dominated the area and a turf war broke out between them. When I say war, I mean war! Gang members were attacked for being in the wrong area and tit-for-tat warfare exploded across the community. Gang members were killed and badly injured leaving local residents terrified.

The Police worked very hard but it was really difficult to get the evidence they needed, because people were too frightened to speak to the Police or to give evidence. The Police Superintendant for the area invited us to meet with him and explained the situation to us. Amidst the laughter from his colleagues, who did not believe that the church could help, he courageously shared his heart for the children of this community and his desire to see them fulfilling their potential. He told us that the "Dog and Gun" pub was at the heart of all that was going on there.

As we prayed, we heard the Lord say we were to drive around that community and pray. So three ladies drove around in my little car and saw for ourselves how heartbreaking the situation was. We were very apprehensive as we were being watched by many of the young men hanging around on the street corners and in the doorways. However, we knew we had the Lord with us and that as long as we were doing what He told us to do, we would be safe.

We prayed at Croxteth Hall, as the land on which the community was now built formed the original Croxteth Hall estate. As we prayed we broke any curses that had originated from there. We then drove around and prayed over every part of the community, releasing love, peace and life etc., until we got to the notorious "Dog and Gun" pub. I have to confess we did not have the courage to get out of the car, so we simply parked the car up for a couple of minutes. We prayed and commanded the pub to be shut, for all the evil activities going on within to be exposed and with substantial evidence for the Police to be able to make the arrests they needed.

Within three weeks the Liverpool Echo's headlines announced the answer to our prayers: "Dog and Gone!" The Police had raided the pub, making eight arrests and seizing a samurai sword, weapons and ammunition, drugs, including heroin, cocaine and cannabis, and money. The pub was not only closed but it was completely demolished and the people who had been arrested were later charged and sent to prison.

Over the following weeks we visited this community several times and called on the Lord to bless them with the regeneration that they desperately needed. Today, most of those homes have now been demolished and beautiful new homes have replaced them. The Police, local Council and other agencies have worked tirelessly to bring a transformation that goes beyond the bricks and mortar.

The crime rate went down dramatically in that area, as did the number of violent attacks. We were thrilled when a documentary starring Martin Kemp was shown on TV. He has made a series of programs visiting some of the worst communities and cities in the world that have been terrorised by gangs. The good news was, that by the time Martin and his TV cameras arrived, most of the gang leaders were safely behind bars.

There are now several churches working across the community and making a really positive difference. A friend of ours, Liam Moore, brought together a choir made up of children from across the schools of the North Liverpool area. They recorded a song called "You're the Voice" and the lyrics were written and originally sung by John Farnham:[7]

> We have the chance to turn the pages over
> We can write what we wanna write
> We gotta make ends meet before we get much older
> We're all someone's daughter
> We're all someone's son
> How long can we look at each other
> Down the barrel of a gun?

> You're the voice, try and understand it
> Make a noise and make it clear
> We're not gonna sit in silence
> We're not gonna live with fear
> This time, you know that we all can stand together
> With the power to be powerful
> Believing, we can make it better
> We're all someone's daughter
> We're all someone's son
> How long can we look at each other?
> Down the barrel of a gun?

This choir and song brought so many families together who would have originally stood on opposite sides of the divide. God is good and He really cares for our communities because the people He loves live there. God longs to bring real transformation and restore what the enemy has stolen from people's lives.

The second story is just as remarkable. In April 2004 we visited Stoke-on-Trent and spoke very briefly in a meeting led by our friends Lloyd Cooke and Robert Mountford. We encouraged the people from Stoke to pray, not only for their own local communities, but also to pray for Liverpool. If Liverpool really was the drugs distribution capital of the UK, then people would be coming from Stoke-on-Trent to get their drugs and vice-versa.

A few days later I got a call from a friend in Manchester. Gary Stretton had been praying and shared with me a vision he had from the Lord. In this vision He had seen a huge ship coming into the docks of Liverpool full of drugs that would have national significance. We prayed together over the telephone and sure enough a few days later in came the ship. The ship's cargo included a large consignment of marble fireplaces that had been hollowed out and filled with 7.2 tonnes of cannabis resin with a street value estimated at £35 million. The Police made five arrests and of those arrests, three men were from Stoke-on-Trent. Sadly one of those men later hung himself whilst in prison.

The Liverpool Echo report quoted DCI Mark Matthews who said, "The significance cannot be underestimated and I am sure this is the biggest seizure of its kind in Merseyside and one of the biggest ever in the country." Since that time Merseyside Police have had great success in their drugs work and have received most of the national awards to mark their success. There are many programs now in place to identify the chaotic and prolific drug takers and to get them help as soon as possible. They are usually offered a holistic package which does not simply deal with their drug habit but looks to give them an opportunity of a whole new life.

Another outcome from these stories and our work with the Police, which did not make it into the newspaper headlines, was the number of Police Officers who became Christians. This included the Police Superintendant who had invited us to pray in the Norris Green and Croxteth communities. A few years ago I was invited to speak at the National Welsh Assembly Prayer Breakfast and this Superintendent came with me. Together we told the story of what God had done as we had worked in partnership to see our communities changed for good.

Today Merseyside Police now have their own Christian support network for personnel called River Force. They also have a wonderful Chaplaincy Service that provides spiritual support and advice to personnel.[8]

We have come a long way and Merseyside is no longer the drug distribution capital of the UK. Crime in the region has dropped substantially and that impacts across the community, as fear and intimidation make room for peace and hope. Businesses and entrepreneurs have believed they can invest in the region and have done so with millions of pounds.

I was honoured to be awarded "Sefton Citizen of the Year 2003" from Merseyside Police and received an award from Safer Merseyside Partnership for the reduction in crime and increase of community safety in 2003. Praise the Lord for His mercy and goodness to us in answering prayer. We give God the glory for all that He has done here and for all the lives that have been turned around.

The Chief Constable of Merseyside Police, Norman Bettison, said this: "It has long been said that the police cannot address the problems in society on our own. That is patently true when one considers the issue of drug abuse. We are grateful for the support and partnership of many different agencies, statutory and voluntary, in addressing this major social menace. We welcome, in particular, the contribution of DrugsNET. Sue and all the team at Merseyside DrugsNET are very active in raising awareness of the problem of drug abuse in the churches in this region and are very successful at engaging the support of so many members of the church-going public. It is a great help to a section of the public to know what they can do to help. It gives everyone a sense of optimism that we can address this problem together. Thank you for all the support you give to the Force. It is appreciated."

If you needed any further encouragement that God answers prayer to transform your community here are some headline quotes from Liverpool for you:

January 2004 - A Government report confirmed that Merseyside Police were winning their battle against crime.

April 2004 - Assistant Prime Minister, John Prescott MP hailed a renaissance in Liverpool's fortunes with growth soaring, unemployment plunging and people moving back to the city centre.

2004 - Liverpool John Lennon Airport was the UK's fastest growing regional airport and Liverpool's £300 million school building program was the biggest in Europe.

July 2004 - we saw £80 million extra funding per year through to 2008 on top of £86 million already announced for housing renewal.

In 2004 - Digby Jones, Director General of the CBI said, "Liverpool is a city whose time has come".

In Summer 2004 the Traveller's Bible which less than 10 years previously had branded Liverpool "a symbol of a nation in decline" now hailed the city's transformation. It said, "Many of England's cities have been revamping themselves, defeating long-held stereotypes. Perhaps the greatest transformation is Liverpool".[9]

In 2004, Council Leader Councillor Mike Storey said "The transformation of Liverpool is staggering. Liverpool's image as a city blighted by unemployment also looks set to be consigned to the history books as its recent record on job creation leaves every other town in the UK in the shade." He hailed the turn-around as an economic miracle but said, "We must not take our foot off the accelerator."

Tony Blair at the Labour Party Conference in 2005 declared the rebirth of Liverpool as one of the proudest achievements of his eight years in office Then in March 2006 Michael Heseltine said, "The spirit of Liverpool has been reborn. It has been transformed dramatically since despairing in 1970's. Today it is the most exciting urban renaissance since Victorian Britain."

There have been many wonderful things since then, including the major redevelopment of the city's shopping area, Liverpool One, covering forty-two acres with new buildings, hotels, restaurants and shops. This opened in 2008 and since then we have seen an extra 50% footfall across the shops and it is reported an extra 100,000 visitors coming to the Albert Docks.

The building of the Liverpool Echo Arena costing £164 million has brought in many millions of pounds and millions of people. Many new hotels have been built creating lots of new jobs as a result of the huge increase in tourism.

A report on www.publications.parliament.uk in March 2011 said "Over the past 10 years, the Liverpool City Region economy has experienced an impressive economic renaissance and provides one of the UK's best examples of regeneration-led transformation.

Visitors will recognise the physical transformation of Liverpool City Centre underpinned by Grosvenor's £1bn investment in Liverpool One, a substantial expansion of the City's commercial and knowledge districts, and new visitor and cultural assets. Significant investment made in new housing. There has also been investment to create significant new employment opportunities. 1999 to 2008, the economy grew fifty percent and the number of jobs grew by 50,600.

Improvements have also been made in education and skills, with the GCSE attainment now matching the UK average (closing a seven percent gap in just five years. As a result of this decade of renaissance, the economy was far more resilient entering the recession than in previous ones and, consequently, has performed relatively better than many other cities across the UK. Over the past ten years, Liverpool City Region has undergone a remarkable transformation. There is a positive and vibrant atmosphere, increased private sector confidence and a clear vision for the future."

On 27th October 2012 The Mirror newspaper reported Steve Rotherham MP as saying "Liverpool is one of the safest metropolitan areas in the country. It's time for people to recognise what's actually happening here and not the nonsense that's peddled by some comedians and others. We need to change the image that far too many people have of the city."

In January 2014 the same Travel Bible Rough Guide named Liverpool as the top UK city and third in the world for people to visit in 2014. They wrote: "What began with the gradual redevelopment of the Albert Dock area has evolved into a full-blown cultural renaissance. Liverpool, once named the world's pop music capital, has rediscovered its mojo. And guess what? It's setting trends again."[9]

Liverpool has also started the construction of a new £300 million deep-water dock to take larger vessels as the port is now so busy. It is said that this will create a further 5,000 jobs that are always welcome.

Work has also started on a £130 million redevelopment of the Stanley Dock area.

We thank God for all that He has done as His people have begun to pray and reach out, all that He is doing and all that will be done in the future.

I want to add that there are many people and ministries across the Liverpool area who have contributed to the shift that is taking place. I honour those who are making such a positive difference.

I hope that reading this causes your faith to arise for what can be done in your community, as you pray and declare God's word.

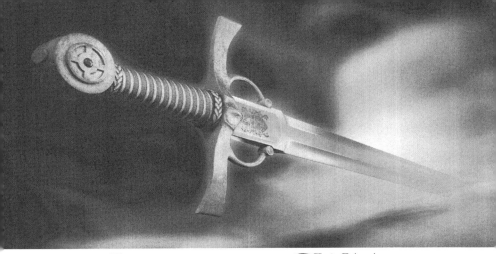

BIRTHING CWM

With a passion for evangelism, developing prayer and the prophetic, my ministry was growing. I helped to lead the ministry team for the visit of evangelist J.John for the Just 10 mission hosted in Liverpool's Anglican Cathedral. Following the success of Just 10, I was invited to lead prayer for Together for the Harvest (TFH) which is an association of churches, organisations and individuals who work together across the Mersey region.

I was also asked to serve on the Board for a project called Merseyfest. This was working towards mobilizing thousands of people to come to Liverpool for a week of mission and outreach, ending with a big concert and festival. I enjoyed networking and pulling in all the favour I had with the Police and the Councils. I was also delighted to see some healthy partnerships developing across the churches. We began to gather people to pray prior to Merseyfest and that was a great learning curve.

I learnt so much from those days; some from the mistakes I made and lots from working with such amazing people. The big thing I learned was about me. I realised I had such an overwhelming passion to see my city filled with Christians fulfilling their destiny. The second thing I learnt was that I was desperate to see multitudes coming to know Jesus as their Saviour and actually Jesus wanted that too. Whilst many leaders were busy with the day to day running of their churches (not a bad thing), they were pleased to settle with Merseyfest just being a successful project. But that was never enough for me, as I saw it as an opportunity for revival to break out.

After a couple of years I knew my time with both TFH and Merseyfest was over. It was a new season and the Lord was calling me to raise up a new team of Christians from across the North West and across the breadth of the church. Our vision initially was to encourage one another to be all that God had destined us to be and to stand in the gap to pray for revival to come again in Liverpool.

We began to gather people one by one as the Lord led us. Each person in the team was hand picked by God Himself and each had different gifts and talents. Today we have a team of people who all compliment one another and our love and unity are our strongest gifts.

I have been leading Community Watchmen Ministries (CWM) since 2002. Our title Community Watchmen Ministries came from our desire to be a healthy "community" of Christians who foster relationships across the church and outside of the church. The very word itself contains the word unity that is so important to us.

"Watchmen" just had to be in our title as that is what we are, people who are watching over our families, communities and nations. Very often the watchmen are intercessors and sometimes they are prophets. Thankfully within CWM we have a mixture of both of those powerful gifts operating.

"The Watchmen opens the gate for Him (that's Jesus), and the sheep hear His voice; He calls His sheep by name and leads them out. When He brings out His own sheep, He goes before them; and the sheep follow Him, for they know His voice." John 10:3-4

We believe that we are called to hear and recognise Jesus' voice and do all that He calls us to do - simple really! This strategy has led us into many exciting adventures with God; life as a Christian is certainly never boring! It is time for us to open the gate and welcome the King of Glory into our lives, churches, ministries, communities and nations, to follow Him out where ever He leads us.

"Ministries" speaks for itself, as the Lord has encouraged us to develop many streams of ministry throughout the UK, Europe and Africa. As previously prophesied, God has led us on many adventures taking us into places of government and giving us opportunities to pray for and give prophetic encouragement to international leaders.

Concerned that we were not seeing our city and region prospering, or people coming to Jesus, we asked God to teach us to pray. Since then being a part of the CWM team has taught us all so much and we have seen many miraculous breakthroughs in issues concerning Liverpool, the UK and the nations. And we are still learning!

By 2004 CWM had grown numerically and spiritually and we had developed a Prayer School, which was prophesied by Martin Scott. Prayer School is an ideal opportunity for people to learn that prayer is an exciting adventure. It is an opportunity for them to be activated in prayer, from the complete beginner to those who have been praying for years. We aim to encourage the church to take hold of prayer in a new and dynamic way in order to see the great commission given to us by Jesus fulfilled.

> *Jesus came to them and said, "All authority in heaven and on earth has been given to me. Therefore go and make disciples of all nations, baptising them in the name of the Father and of the Son and of the Holy Spirit, and teaching them to obey everything I have commanded you. And surely I am with you always, to the very end of the age."*
> Matthew 28:18-20

It is important that we all understand the answers to these questions:

Who is God?

Who are we?

What is our destiny and why are we here?

We provide several teaching sessions complete with real life inspiring illustrations and testimonies. Our teaching is very practical starting with "Intimacy with God" and going through to "Transforming our Communities".

Prayer School is very flexible working around the needs of the host church or churches. The feedback has been excellent with many church leaders telling us it has changed the life of their church completely.

Reverend Charles Finnie from Burnfoot Parish Church, Hawick, said: "You bring a message which for some could be extremely complicated and you present it in a simple, straightforward manner, with huge heaven originated effects. The fact that in my experience whenever you guys turn up something of God comes as well, suggests not only have you something of God's favour, but also there is a consistent anointing on you for what God is continuing to do. I pray that you continue to seek and know His revelation for your own lives, for Liverpool, and for sharing with the church across the UK."

We speak at conferences, provide leadership training and support, plus we are involved with many international prayer initiatives. We also speak and minister regionally, nationally and internationally for other ministries, churches and networks.

CWM used to meet in Strawberry Fields; yes the Strawberry Fields that John Lennon sang about. Then the Lord began to tell me that He was going to give me a building. I kept saying "but Lord I don't want a building, as we don't need one and it would tie us down". Eventually the Lord said "Are you going to ask me about this building?"

So as a team we prayed and then sat quietly, asking God to describe the building to us. Each person wrote down the description of the building they could see. We then shared what we had seen and wrote down the description that was common to us all. The building we all saw was amazing and so much better than we would have ever dared to ask God for. There was only one problem; we did not know where it was! So I asked the Lord to show us where it was as Liverpool is a big place. Immediately an image of the building came to my mind and I knew exactly where it was.

The building was just about to be bought by friends of ours who lead a Baptist church in Aintree near Liverpool. There is an amazing story here in how God provided for them and how they welcomed us into their building. Today we have a wonderful partnership as we have our office and prayer space in their church building called The Hope Centre.

I would like to honour Pastor John Kearns who has become a great friend of ours. John is the minister of the thriving church at The Hope Centre.

When we moved into The Hope Centre, the Lord was waiting for us and He immediately challenged us to step up a level. So instead of meeting once a fortnight we began to meet twice a week. The Lord met with us very powerfully and we soon realised that something special was happening.

We were really enjoying God's presence and the team was growing and developing wonderfully. We often pray about governmental and strategic issues. We pray for church leaders and market place leaders. Everything that happens in our office stays in our office, as confidentiality is essential. However we knew that we needed to share what we were experiencing of the presence of God with a wider group.

With that in mind in January 2009 Big PUSH was born. The Lord gave us the name and it comes from that moment when a woman is giving birth and the midwife says, "It's time to give a Big PUSH". That Big PUSH delivers the new baby and we believe we are called to PUSH through to see REVIVAL delivered. It is also a military term when the army gives a big PUSH to see the enemy pushed back from the land. So Big PUSH is a great description for our monthly gatherings of Christians, who all have a desire and a passion to see revival and transformation breaking out.

The Big PUSH has been a very significant journey for Christians from different styles and networks of church, choosing to gather together to praise, worship, prophecy and cry out to God for the release of a major move of God once again across our land. Just like Hannah who had to arise and PUSH through all the discouragements to birth her son Samuel, who was born to change the nation, we believe it is time for Christians to PUSH in to God together for the sake of our region and our nations.

We have seen over 750 men and women come along to the Big PUSH, many coming regularly and some travelling several hours to be with us. The furthest distance travelled has been New Zealand, plus we have had guests from many other nations including South Africa, Uganda, Ghana, Nigeria, Kenya, USA and Belgium. Wow!

The CWM Team love to teach, empower and activate the church and have a strong anointing to bring breakthrough. We provide training, empowering and activation for people in prayer and also in learning to hear God's voice (the prophetic) and give opportunities for people to be mobilised effectively. CWM are a team of ordinary men and woman who are learning to walk with an amazing, awesome and extraordinary God.

We also think it is important to provide a safe place for Leaders to come to receive prophetic prayer ministry and encouragement. We supply a recorded copy to them of all that has been prayed and prophesied. If required we also meet with church and ministry leadership teams on site.

We have undertaken several interesting and exciting prayer journeys taking us to the heart of the governments of the United States of America, Belgium, Germany, Republic of Ireland, Northern Ireland, Wales, the Isle of Man and Uganda and many other places.

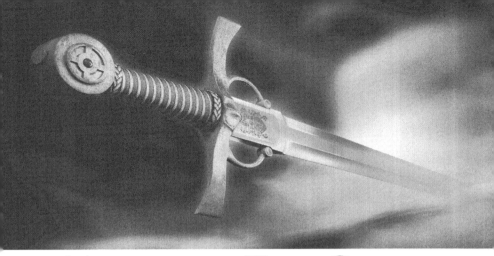

MANNING THE GATES

He also stationed gatekeepers at the gates of the Lord's temple so that no one who was in any way unclean might enter. 2 Chronicles 23:19

One of the things we have done has been to learn how to be good watchmen and gatekeepers. We watch over the region to ensure that nothing evil moves through the gates and as much as possible only good things can move in or out. As you can imagine, there have been lots of challenges. Here is the story of one of those challenges.

The Bible tells us that we should have no other gods but Him. So when I heard that the Dalai Llama had been invited to visit the Liverpool Anglican Cathedral and Liverpool Town Hall, I was appalled. The Dalai Llama is the head of the Tibetan Buddhists and everywhere he goes there is a release of demonic spirits. As we prayed one evening in the Liverpool Anglican Cathedral, I heard the Lord say that we needed to repent that he had been invited. Also we had to pray that the Dalai Llama's voice would not be heard and the demonic powers would have no access into Liverpool.

I gently shared what I believed the Lord was saying and suggested that if people wanted to join with me they could come to the altar to repent on behalf of the people of Liverpool. I did not say on behalf of the Anglican Church, the Bishop or the leaders. Those who did not feel they could join with me were free to stay and worship the Lord. Many came to the altar and quietly knelt and prayed. There was no fuss and when we finished praying at the altar, we simply continued with the rest of the Prayer Gathering.

Two things happened:

1) The Dalai Llama visited Liverpool and as he came out of Liverpool Town Hall, he walked over to the crowd waiting outside. He went across to an elderly man in a wheelchair and spoke to him quietly, before being driven off to his next location. The media swooped on the man eager to hear what the Dalai Llama had said. The man simply said, "I don't know, I am completely deaf in that ear!" We felt this was a real sign to us that God had answered our prayers and had silenced the voice of the Dalai Llama just as we had prayed.

2) I was called in to see two church leaders and told that a complaint had been made about me praying prayers of repentance and that I needed to issue an apology. I was really saddened that the very people who should have been leading the way spiritually were demanding an apology from me. I really did not want to offend anyone, but I could not see how I could apologise without offending God. The challenge was would I be a man pleaser or a God pleaser?

I prayed, asking the Lord what I should do. I was listening to a Godfrey Birtill song and as the words "stand and I will stand with you" rang out I sensed the Lord saying that if I would stand for righteousness He would stand with me. I felt the Leaders put me under a lot of pressure to apologise but in the end I simply said, "I am sorry that anyone has been offended by my prayers but I cannot apologise for praying them." I knew that if I did so it would nullify the prayers and give my blessing to the Dalai Llama. I have nothing against the man but stand totally opposed to all the demonic activity that travels with him. They were not happy with me at all.

146

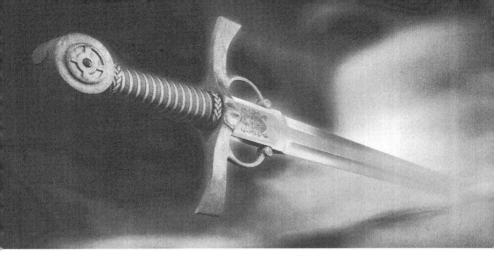

A Painful Shift

Steve and I had faithfully and served in our church for over twenty-one years and I had been a part of the Leadership Team for several years. I never expected to move from there. I really believed I would be there until Jesus came again or until I was carried out in a box! So what happened next really shocked and devastated us.

I know that I am never going to be a person who loves to settle; after all I am a pioneer, a visionary and prophetic too. There is always more available for us as God's children. My passion is to see every person fulfilling their God-given potential and to see our churches engaged in building God's kingdom.

However our greatest strengths can be our greatest areas of vulnerability. If people do not want to change, someone like myself can be very irritating! I know that and try very hard not to irritate people too much. I had a frustrating year at church and felt rejected and bullied. That was when the prophecy and the extravagant fire came.

In the summer of 2007 I was given a prophetic word that simply said that God was going to move us and move us very quickly. I had no idea at all what that referred to or what might be ahead. However within three weeks we discovered everything was about to move and change dramatically.

Suddenly things came to a head when it was decided to use the Freedom in Christ materials for the Leadership Team. This is all about being honest and dealing with painful issues that are stumbling blocks for the growth of the church. It suddenly dawned on me that this would put me in a very difficult position. I knew the deception I was being forced to live with regarding Mary and Tom, would not only be affecting our lives and the lives of Mary's family, but also the life of the church.

All my bible studies had led me to believe that the way things had been dealt with had been wrong e.g. Abraham and Sarah in Genesis 12:10-19 and Genesis 20 and the New Testament model of the fruit of deception was seen with Ananias and Sapphira in Acts 5. In each case deception resulted in sickness and even death and that is really scary.

It would have been easy to just ignore what had happened but I was afraid of compromising, as that would defeat the object of the appointment in the first place. I found myself in an impossible position so I decided to take advice and to step down temporarily (possibly permanently) from the Leadership Team, until I was sure of how to progress and that way I would not have to attend the SYCF appointment.

One of the Elders came to see me, to talk to me and to try to understand why I was considering leaving the Leadership Team. He could see that something was clearly wrong. So in the end I was persuaded to tell him what had happened. Before I knew it the whole thing had imploded and we were left with no alternative but to leave the church. Prior to leaving we wrote to the Elders, to honour them and ask if we could meet them before we left. We also asked if we could leave with a blessing, but both our requests were denied.

We were left feeling hurt, bewildered and stunned by all that happened. I am sure that we did not get everything right and that we made mistakes. However, we were not even given an opportunity to hear what they thought we had done wrong or, if so how to put that right. We found it difficult leaving under those circumstances and we could not tell others why we were leaving and therefore gossip was rife. Consequently some people avoided us and it was as though we had left the planet and not just one part of God's church. We found that some of our relationships with people whom we had considered as friends have since drifted apart. We felt like few people seemed to care that we had been left for dead. I guess these are the times when you find out who your real friends are.

On a positive note we heard that eventually Tom did tell his Dad the truth and thankfully their relationship was not damaged.

All of this happened when Steve was away and I was completely broken. It was not the first time I had been battered and left for dead, as all the old feelings of rejection and old insecurities surfaced. It is during these times that you start to believe that it is all your fault and you are just a bad person. I understood why Job had said:

"Why did you bring me out of the womb? I wish I had died before any eye saw me. If only I had never come into being, or had been carried straight from the womb to the grave!" Job 10:18-19

When people are wounded in church or they have left the church wounded and battered, we often treat them like the religious people did in the story of the "Good Samaritan". People usually walk by and do nothing to help. We find it difficult to believe that our Leaders can do anything wrong and so the wounded person must have done something to "deserve it". That was the shocking truth we discovered when we were wounded and left for dead by some people in God's church.

We were left with no alternative but to walk away from a church filled with people we had loved and still love. We felt like we had become exiled. We were walking through the extravagant fire but we were not walking alone, Jesus walked through the fire with us. He understood our pain; after all, Jesus was rejected by His own people too.

We have since encountered so many other people who had similar stories. In the midst of our communities there are many who have been wounded by their experience of church, some who have now opted out of church altogether. Something I am sure breaks God's heart.

Please hear my heart, as I really believe that God still wants to pour out His Spirit in a mighty way through this church and I love them. I want to honour the Pastor, the Eldership and all those who have had a very positive influence in our lives and we choose to hold nothing against them. I also believe that it is very important for us to bless others and I willingly continue to pray for God's best for them.

It is not just what happens to us that matters in our journey with the Lord, but also how we respond to what happens. I was totally crushed, but as I kept my focus on the Lord I was not destroyed! I came to realise that others in the story may never be open to reconciliation, but I had to allow Jesus to heal me and my family. I needed to extend forgiveness even if they never asked for it, because that is what Jesus did; "Father forgive them they know not what they do".

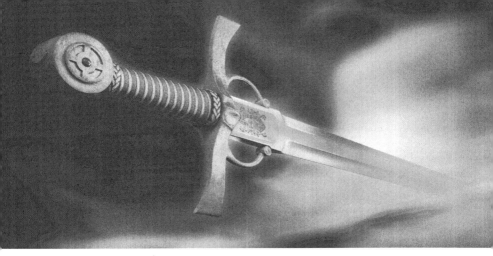

ANOINTING

Ann Graham Lotz is an amazing woman of God and in her book "Wounded by God's people" she writes, "Don't let the memories and mistreatment, the words and the wounds, the jealousy and the hypocrisy, the deceit and the dishonesty, the cheap talk and the inconsistent walk, the meanness, the unkindness, rudeness, pridefullness, selfishness, sinfulness, injustice, and unfairness of people from your past creep into the present and ruin the promise of blessing and hope for the future."[10] Good words indeed!

As time went on, we came to understand that the move was actually very good for us and was part of God's plan for the next phase of our lives. It changed Steve and I, as we recognised just how arrogant and insular we had been as Christians. Moving church widened our understanding of God and His beautiful church. It also set us free from the deception, which had overshadowed our lives for too many years. The shadow that had loomed over our lives was gone and we were free.

I love these verses:

> "For my determined purpose is that I may know Him [that I may progressively become more deeply and intimately acquainted with

Him, perceiving and recognising and understanding the wonders of his Person more strongly and more clearly], and that I may in that same way come to know the power outflowing from his resurrection which it exerts over believers], and that I may so share his sufferings as to be continually transformed [in spirit into His likeness even] to His death, [in the hope]" Philippians 3:10 (Amplified)

"I do not consider, brethren, that I have captured and made it my own [yet]; but one thing I do [it is my one aspiration]: forgetting what lies behind and straining forward to what lies ahead, I press on toward the goal to win the [supreme and heavenly] prize to which God in Christ Jesus is calling us upward." Philippians 3:13-14 (Amplified)

Community Watchmen Ministries have gone from strength to strength, despite all that has happened. I would almost dare to say that it has developed so much because I have allowed the extravagant fire to come and I have not just survived but thrived. I have never been in the fire by myself because the Lord Himself has been as good as His word and He has never left me or forsaken me.

It has not been easy and there has been no room for anger, bitterness or unforgiveness. It has been essential to deal with any issues quickly and as thoroughly as possible.

Sadly there have been other times too, when the fire has come again, but that's life! We all have times when the fire gets almost too hot for us to bear. It is in those times that it is important for us to see it as the extravagant fire that God allows to enrich us and increase the level of the anointing we walk in.

Our testimony has been that the new life that comes after the fire has done its work, has been truly amazing. You can read some of the incredible stories for yourself in my next book. I have to say that we are very ordinary people but as we have learned to walk hand in hand with God, we have experienced the most incredible things and witnessed the most outrageous fruit. In the next book, you will read of how the Lord opened doors for us to go into the most surprising places like the White House, the Pentagon and many other places of government around the world. You can also read the tragic story of the Hillsborough disaster and our journey to enable the truth to be revealed.

As you have read about some of my journey I hope that the Lord has spoken to you. Pause for a few moments for reflection. What stage are you at?

- Are you struggling? Do you feel that you are not thriving and you are overwhelmed with dead wood and rot?
- Are you in the midst of the fire?
- Has the fire been extinguished but you are shattered and feeling as if there is nothing left?
- Are you seeing the new shoots of a brand new start beginning to arise?
- Are you thriving?

What ever the stage you are in, choose to focus on Jesus and allow Him to bring you into all that He has destined for you.

Meanwhile my prayer for you is that:

- You will really know how much God loves you.
- You will be a victor and not a victim.
- You will welcome the extravagant fire of God that comes to burn up all that stops you flourishing.
- You will experience new life and growth.
- You will walk in the amazing destiny that the Lord has created you for.

And finally a word of encouragement that could have come from God Himself, but instead was spoken to one of my heroes:

"You are Braver than you believe
Stronger than you seem,
And Smarter than you think"

Christopher Robin to Winnie the Pooh![11]

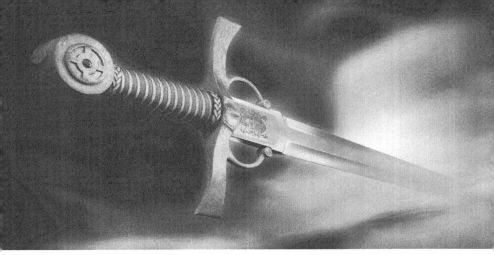

REFERENCES

Chapter 1

Freedom in Christ Ministries   www.ficm.org.uk

Bethel Redding   http://store.ibethel.org

Messenger International   http://messengerinternational.org/
ukstore/

Joyce Meyer Ministries   http://www.joycemeyer.org/
Bookstore.aspx

Chapter 10

1.   "Footprints" by Carolyn Joyce Carty

Chapter 13

2   Don't Make History Change the Future; Matt Summerfield;
Chief Executive of Urban Saints; Kindle

3   Culture of Honour; Danny Lee Silk; Destiny Image; 1 edition
(1 December 2009)

4   Blessings and Curses - you can choose; Derek Prince; Chosen
Books; 3Rev Ed edition (1 September 2006)

Chapter 15

5   Freedom in Christ; T Anderson and Steve Goss

Chapter 19

6   Transformation Series: www.sentinelgroup.org

7   You're the voice; John Farnham; 1987

8   http://www.coact.org.uk/pdf/WorkForPolice.pdf

9   The Traveller's Bible;

Chapter 23

10   Wounded by God's people; Ann Graham Lotz; Zondervan
       (21 August 2013)

11   Christopher Robin to Winnie the Pooh; A A Milne

SUE SINCLAIR

Sue Sinclair is married to Steve and has two children. Sue has served on the Sefton Local Strategic Partnership for eight years, as Prayer Co-ordinator for Christian networks Together For the Harvest and Merseyfest for several years as well as playing an active role in local church leadership.

Sue is a visionary and has pioneered many new ministries within the church and reaching out into the community. Sue has led CommUNITY Watchmen Ministries (CWM) since 2002; based in Merseyside CWM consists of Christians from across the North West and across the breadth of the Church.

CWM reaches out into the local communities, the region, the nation and across the nations. They minister throughout the UK, Europe and Africa. God has led them on many adventures taking them into places of government and giving them opportunities to pray for and give prophetic encouragement to international government Ministers.

Sue and the CWM team love to teach, empower and activate the Church and have a strong anointing to bring breakthrough. Sue is just an ordinary woman who is learning to walk with an amazing and awesome God.

www.cwmprayer.com

Extravagant Adventures

Synopsis

EXTRAVAGANT ADVENTURES is Sue's second book and describes what happens when God takes ordinary people and uses them to do amazing things. Life with Jesus can be an exhilarating adventure, when God speaks to you and you simply do what He tells you to do, anything can happen.

This book tells of the exploits of Sue and the Community Watchmen Ministries Team (CWM). Coming from Liverpool, a gateway place, they have learned to follow as the Lord has opened many doors into places of government and into the nations.

It tells the story of how four pieces of coal led them on a journey to Northern Ireland, Belgium and the USA. Each of those nations visited included trips into the their corridors of power.

EXTRAVAGANT ADVENTURES will raise your levels of faith and confidence in what God can do through very ordinary people. You will read miraculous stories of God transforming cities and shifting nations.

Publication Date: Spring 2015